LEADERSHIP EXCELLENCE IN MARKETING AND SALES

DR GAJANAN SHIRKE

Contents

Acknowledgements — *v*

About Book — *vii*

About The Author — *ix*

Index — *xi*

1. Coaching Salespeople — 1

2. High Performance Teams Inside The Company — 7

3. High Performance Teams Remote Workplace — 12

4. In Person Sales — 15

5. Internet Marketing Fundamentals — 17

6. Marketing Basics — 22

7. Media And Public Relations — 28

8. Motivating Your Sales Team — 37

9. Overcoming Sales Objections — 43

10. Presentation Skills — 50

11. Proposal Writing — 54

12. Prospecting And Lead Generation — 58

13. Sales Fundamentals — 65

14. Social Media Marketing — 73

15. Top Sales Secrets — 77

Acknowledgements

I would like to express a special debt of gratitude to my wife Rajeshree and my two daughters Rupeshi & Kavya, my teammates and superior leaders who encourages me to write.

About Book

This book makes a much needed contribution to what young leaders know about the Sales and Marketing role. It offers great insights into the different management challenges leader's faces, and it provides readers with a rich array of data regarding the mental, emotional, social, and physical adjustments accompanying one's transition to leadership role. The book is an ideal pick for young managers, entrepreneurs, and graduate students who wish to acquaint themselves with all the aspects of sales management. It is also an excellent teaching aid for the academic fraternity and industry professionals who teach sales and marketing management courses.

About The Author

Dr Gajanan Shirke, a hotel consultant, has years of extensive experience in the hospitality industry. His thirst for learning and aspiration to become a multi-faceted expert in the hotel industry helped him rise from employment to becoming an independent professional in the hospitality sector. Since his last assignment as General Manager at Kamat Hotels, he has become a renowned hotel consultant with a proven track record of developing, training and growing some of the best-known hotels, restaurants and fast-food joints in the Indian market. He was appointed as an expert consultant for The Eighth meeting of the Board of Studies for Hotel Management & Catering Technology. He is a visiting faculty at various Hotel Management Colleges and has trained over a thousand hospitality professionals. He has completed numerous pre and post opening hotel consultancies in India and overseas.

In order to spread his extensive knowledge to aspiring hotel professionals, Gajanan has penned a large number of books spanning different segments of the hospitality industry. Starting from his first book 'Bar Management and Operations' published in 2010, he has written 46 books including Hospitality Management, Food and Beverage Management, Hotel Engineering Management, Front Office Management, Hotel Housekeeping Management, The Cookery Trilogy: Advance Cookery Theory, The Cookery Trilogy: Foundation of Cookery, The Cookery Trilogy: The Basic Cookery Book, Hotel Sales and Marketing, Hospitality Industry Accounting & Fundamentals, Customer Interaction Excellence in Hospitality, History of Indian Cuisine – Volume 1, History of Indian Cuisine – Volume 2, Hotel Owner's Manual, Hotel Security & Prevention, Training Manager's Manual, Exceptional Service In Hospitality Six Sigma Way, etc.

Index

1. Coaching Salespeople
2. High Performance Teams Inside the Company
3. High Performance Teams Remote Workplace
4. In Person Sales
5. Internet Marketing Fundamentals
6. Marketing Basics
7. Media and Public Relations
8. Motivating your sales team
9. Overcoming Sales Objections
10. Presentation Skills
11. Proposal Writing
12. Prospecting and lead generation
13. Sales Fundamentals
14. Social Media Marketing
15. Top Sales Secrets

CHAPTER ONE

Coaching Salespeople

A good sales coach unlocks serious revenue potential — and the data proves it. Effective sales coaching not only helps reps improve productivity and efficiency, it can increase sales performance by 8%. The bad news is that many sales managers find coaching a difficult skill to master – especially in environments where reps are increasingly remote and are being asked to do more with less time and fewer resources. If you're not getting the support you need to effectively coach your sales team, don't despair. These 10 sales coaching tips are easy to implement with many of the tools already at your disposal, and are effective for both in-person and remote teams. Effective sales coaching is iterative, individualized, and inclusive. It's designed to reinforce positive behavior or correct negative behavior. Typically part of each sales rep's daily or weekly routine, sales coaching is focused on skills and techniques rather than numbers. A sales coach uses data to monitor individual rep performance to identify areas for improvement and reinforce behaviors that lead to success. They also develop coaching initiatives that build confidence in reps by providing them with the tools and skills they need to succeed.

Most importantly, a sales coach creates an environment of success that empowers employees to feel as though they can grow, contribute to team success and take accountability for their performance. Becoming an effective sales coach comes from experience, but there are various sales coaching programs that can help you learn how to build successful teams that consistently meet and exceed quotas. It's important to note that a sales coach is focused on the individual development of a sales representatives, which is what differentiates the role from a sales manager.

What *doesn't* fall under the sales coaching umbrella?

- Telling salespeople exactly what to do (rather than giving them the end goal and letting them figure out the specifics).
- Giving the same advice to every single person.
- Ignoring individual motivators, strengths, and weaknesses.

Benefits of Sales Coaching: As highlighted in the introduction, sales coaching has a proven, positive impact on your bottom line. But win rates aren't the only reason you should coach your sales reps.

Sales coaching improves employee retention rates: Representative turnover is a notorious problem in sales. While burnout or a bigger salary elsewhere will always tempt some, professional development opportunities will motivate many others to stay. 9 in 10 employees say professional development is "important" or "very important," and 4 in 10 specifically want in-house programs.

Sales coaching gives you an opportunity to share best practices: When you notice one rep is using a strategy to great success, you can immediately teach the rest of your team to do the same thing, similar to how a HubSpot sales rep's success with video prospecting spread throughout his team. Think of sales coaching as a rising tide that lifts all boats.

Sales coaching maximizes your investment in sales training: Companies spend billions per year on sales training, but research shows most of the curriculum doesn't stick. Effective sales training relies on consistent, long-term reinforcement — which the sales manager can achieve through sales coaching.

Coaching Models: There are hundreds of different sales coaching models. Many managers are less than enthused about them — and it's not too difficult to understand why.

Some coaching models are designed for any manager with reports, rather than a sales manager and their reps. But sales is an incredibly distinct profession. It requires a unique coaching model. If you're considering a generic model, you'll likely struggle trying to adapt it to your team. Some models only work with specific methodologies. That can be frustrating if you don't like the model you're supposed to use. Luckily, you can always create a hybrid of your prescribed coaching model — one you're more enthusiastic about.

And remember, some models are *overly* structured. Look for something flexible that you can use with different sales processes — that way, if you change your strategy, you won't need a brand-new coaching model. If you aren't sure if a coaching model is a good fit, ask your team. Their feedback matters most; after all, they are the ones who should benefit. You might use an employee feedback tool, or conduct an internal survey, to get this information from your team. Now that you have a better understanding of what sales coaching is and why it's important, let's look at some sales coaching techniques you can implement.

Coaching Goals: It's best to adapt your sales coaching goals to align with the specific needs of your business. For example, if your company aims to achieve 100,000 in revenue per quarter, you should adapt your coaching to drive reps to meet that goal. However, here are some standard sales coaching goals and objectives that can relate to every company:

- Strengthen relationships with sales reps and create an environment of trust.
- Provide consistent and ongoing coaching and feedback to reps, so they understand their performance and are aware of areas that need improvement.
- Work with sales reps to develop the professional skills they need to succeed by providing them with the necessary tools and resources.
- Build confidence in reps and their ability to succeed by calling out behaviors that lead to success.
- Inspire reps to take responsibility and accountability for their sales performance.

Desired Outcomes: Effective sales coaching inspires professional development and is the key to ensuring your business can reach its revenue goals. Specific outcomes can vary, but these are common desired outcomes of sales coaching:

- Sales reps are productive and successful independently, and guidance is only needed when data shows that performance is falling. However,
- Sales reps are accountable, take ownership of their daily activities, and know when to ask for help.
- Targets are consistently met and exceeded, and the business is on track to meet revenue goals.
- Pipelines are filled with qualified, relevant leads.
- Deals have a higher win rate.
- Sales cycle length is not too exhaustive.

- Retention rates for sales reps are high.

Coaching Plan: As mentioned above, the sales coaching program that you design to lead your teams should depend on your business goals. However, there are a few key elements that should be present in every sales coaching plan.

1. **Onboarding Plan:** Let the reps know everything they need to know about joining your sales org, like a training schedule, key people to know, and required tools and resources that will help them succeed.

2. **High-Level Goals:** Outline what is expected of sales reps in their current position. This can be broken down in goals that are to be met monthly, quarterly, or after a determined period of days.

3. **Check-in Schedule:** Let reps know when you will be meeting with them to asses their progress towards meeting those goals.

While these are the most important aspects of your coaching plan, the sections you include should go in-depth and provide reps with as much information as possible. Below we'll provide a sales coaching plan template that can be customized to meet your business needs and help you lead your teams to success.

Give personal rewards: Individual prizes should be tied to a specific rep's goals. For example, if a rep is working on increasing their call-to-meetings rate, you might say you'll take them to a nice lunch once they improve by X %.

Experiment with new coaching practices and resources: There are many sales coaching techniques and tools available today don't be afraid to experiment with them. Every team and individual are different meaning, no sales coaching techniques are always going to be one-size-fits-all. Learn about what's going to work best for your reps and their needs and ask each rep for their feedback on your coaching style in your one-on-one meetings. Then, stick with these tactics until you reach a point in time when you need to reevaluate their effectiveness and impact.

Practice with multiple coaching scenarios: As a sales manager, it's your job to prepare and practice with multiple coaching scenarios. Your team is bound to evolve and the people on it are going to change (in terms of their skillset but also rep turnover). Stay efficient and effective in regards to coaching by preparing for different scenarios — this way, you'll be ready to assist and teach reps with different needs and areas for improvement at any point in time.

Additionally, you might notice you have several people who need the same type of coaching in a specific problem area. In this case, you can prepare with training and information around that topic and share it among the group. Or, if one rep is struggling in a specific area, you may have a prepared outline of a plan you can then tailor towards their needs — then, you can use it again in the future with another rep.

Have the hard conversations: Many sales reps struggle to meet their potential because of the inevitable prospect push-back ... and the dreaded word, *No*. But most reps work their way through this discomfort with practice. With the sales reps you're coaching, role play some uncomfortable scenarios and hard conversations, practicing some common objections. Once reps get more comfortable hearing those objections and responding accordingly, they'll be better equipped to face them on real sales calls.

Give more positive than negative feedback: For as many pieces of constructive criticism you provide to your sales reps, give twice as much positive reinforcement. Not only does this help maintain morale, but it also allows sales reps to recognize what they're doing right — and hopefully encourages them to repeat and build on that behavior.

Build trust with authentic stories: For sales coaching to work, sales managers must earn reps' trust. This allows the individual to be open about performance challenges. The best way to start is by sharing personal and professional stories. These anecdotes should be authentic, revealing fault and weakness as much as success. There are two goals here: support reps with relatable stories so they know they're not struggling alone, and let them know there are ways to address and overcome challenges. For example, a seasoned manager might share details about their first failed sales call as a cautionary tale – highlighting poor preparation, aggressive posturing, and lack of empathy during the conversation. This would be followed by steps the manager took to fix these mistakes, like call rehearsing and early-stage research into the prospect's background, business, position, and pain points.

Encourage self-evaluation: When doing post-call debriefs or skill assessments – or just coaching during one-on-ones – it's critical to have the salesperson self-evaluate. As a sales manager, you may only be with the rep one or two days a month. Given this disconnect, the goal is to encourage the sales rep to evaluate their own performance and build self-improvement goals around these observations. There are two important components to this. First, avoid jumping directly into feedback during your interactions. Relax and take a step back; let the sales rep self-evaluate. Effective sales coaches don't set focus areas for their salespeople; they let reps set this for themselves. During your one-on-ones, see if there's an important area each rep wants to focus on and go with their suggestion (recommending adjustments as needed to ensure their goals align with those of the company). This creates a stronger desire to improve as it's the rep who is making the commitment. Less effective managers will pick improvement goals for their reps, then wonder why they don't get buy-in.

Focus on one improvement at a time: For sales coaching to be effective, work with the rep to improve one area at a time instead of multiple areas simultaneously. With the former, you see acute focus and measurable progress. With the latter, you end up with frustrated, stalled-out reps pulled in too many directions.

CHAPTER TWO

High Performance Teams inside the Company

Sales success depends on having a successful sales team. A successful sales team, naturally, depends on both effective sales management and the performance of its salespeople. And salespeople who excel share essential professional traits. High-performing sales teams don't become that way by accident. They are assembled and developed over time by dedicated sales managers who understand the key drivers of selling success. As a sales leader, if you understand what makes a successful sales team, you are going to be in a much better position to emphasize these qualities and take your team to that next level.

No doubt, every business is a unique case and needs a personalized approach when increasing their sales team efficiency. However, after years of experience helping our clients to improve their sales process, CIENCE has differentiated certain patterns that are common for high-performing sales teams. Here are five of these essential characteristics and behaviors, which you absolutely need to adapt in your business.

Achieving high win rates: High-performing sales teams first and foremost

- Setting and maintaining ambitious targets
- Challenging themselves to resolve buyer problems
- Concentrating on the delivery of high-value solutions

While several other factors contribute to conversion efficiency, high performers necessarily set top-ambitious goals. If you don't challenge your team to strive for top-level productivity, they will never take the steps necessary to grow and develop the abilities to reach them. The highest performers reach their high goals by prospecting to higher-value sales leads, often using account-based marketing.

Improve sales development processes: One of the most integral points of differentiation between high-performing sales teams and average performers is a constant emphasis on improving the selling process. Sales leaders spend much of their time looking for growth opportunities, developing effective coaching strategies, and implementing training activities aligned with the specific areas in which their team or individual representatives need to grow. Businesses can provide greater opportunity for their sales teams to thrive by allowing them to focus on closing deals and removing the need for prospecting, which can be easily outsourced to a third party. By providing your team qualified opportunities in the form of qualified sales leads or even appointments, you enable them to use their time and energy more efficiently, paying more attention to what is most profitable for your business.

As gaps are detected in your sales process, managers on high-performing sales teams invest in resources that help your team. Thus, high-growth companies with more top performers invest way more effort in deploying more technologies and sales engagement platforms (SEPs) than laggard businesses. As you develop the abilities and performance capabilities of team members, continue to raise the bar. Being a high performer means never settling into a comfort zone.

Maintain your team's motivation: Understanding your team's motivation plays a critical role in the sustained success of salespeople. Its importance is often overlooked. In many cases, at the very beginning of their career, sales representatives feel inspired by the new beginnings and selling challenges. However, when the honeymoon phase wears off, some salespeople lose their grip. In high-performing sales teams, their leaders sustain salespeople's motivation intensity over the long term. It is in our human nature to have ups and downs, and highs and lows. Companies who expect their salespeople to both nurture and close more deals daily experience greater turnover and burnout among their teams. In fact, many of the most successful salespeople failed during the periods of their career where they were expected to prosper. You need to nurture the habits of top sales performers in your team and let them do what they are best at. Understand the factors that drive your team to overcome adversity and stay focused in the long term. Don't make the success of the salesperson limited to their weakest ability.

Deliver real value to your prospects: The ability to understand the full value of the solutions you sell and to articulate that value to buyers can increase sales productivity. The only thing that separates your business from low-price sellers is the superior quality of the products and services your company provides. If buyers don't see this enhanced value, your price points may seem too high. Value comes in many different forms, including style, durability, dependability, reliability, and compelling differentiating features, along with a multitude of service and support features. Top sales teams clearly recognize the full value of the benefits they provide, which positively affects their revenues. A major component of achieving this is by first understanding the problems and deep-level frustrations experienced by an individual prospect. A customer-centric attitude is inherent among high-performing sales teams.

Focus on nurturing new accounts: Lead nurturing is a common pain point for any sales organization. The ability to efficiently convert interested prospects into buyers is crucial for the survival of your business. However, top-level sales teams move beyond just nurturing leads. They focus on nurturing new accounts. Generating one-time sales deals isn't a strategy that is going to lead to high efficiency and profits. In many cases, the first sale may not even cover the acquisition costs required to get the account. Therefore, it is necessary to focus on repeat purchases, loyalty, and long-term retention to build a powerful profit engine.

Nurturing accounts begins with a one-hundred percent follow-through on delivering the solutions promised. Complete fulfillment may include delivery of tangible products, installation, training and support, and ongoing customer service. Follow-up communication is equally important. Intentional, regular phone and e-mail communication with clients demonstrate that you care about their experiences. Building this trust leads to renewals and reorders, as well as add-on sales, cross-sells, and referrals.

Develop Your Sales Team High Performers: The list of major factors that separate high-performing sales teams from average ones isn't overly long. However, the lengths to which the top teams implement these key elements of sales strategy are impressive. The most important quality that defines high performers is that they commit to delivering value and achieving high win rates. They seek out every opportunity to improve the selling processes stage by stage.

Constantly iterate: It can be tempting to keep doing the same things you're used to doing, especially if they're working. But high-performing sales teams are constantly refining, changing processes, and iterating in order to take things to the next level. This can be a tricky endeavor, and can be uncomfortable for those who aren't used to rapid change. But regularly tweaking your processes can pay dividends, as long as you're willing to change, and, occasionally, to fail.

Hold your sales reps accountable: For sales representative, accountability is a double-edged sword. We all want to produce, but when we're not doing well, more pressure can be frustrating, and, for some people, have the opposite of its intended effect. That being said, top-performing sales teams hold their reps accountable, letting poor performers go when working with them to help them improve hasn't paid off. It's an unpleasant aspect of running a sales team, and few people enjoy this aspect of the business, but accountability is a necessary aspect of sales, even if it's the most difficult one.

HANDLING REJECTION: It takes an average of eight cold calls just to reach a prospect, and once you do, there's no guarantee that they will buy what you're selling. Sales is a hard game, and 80% of sales require at least five follow-up calls in order to close the deal. As a result, your team needs to be prepared to handle rejection if you want to keep morale high and keep closing those deals. What makes a great sales team is knowing how to cope with knock-backs and not letting it affect their motivation. If you want to create a team that does just that, then consider holding training sessions and review meetings where you can talk through these problems and handle them professionally. Once more members of your team start doing this, everybody else will follow by example.

MASTERED TOOLS AND TECH: To make the most of this, make sure your team have all the tools they need to thrive: train them on analytics and sales acceleration tools, as well as teaching them the right way to reach out to potential leads via new channels like social media and mobile phones. Giving them an excellent understanding of CRM software is also a must, but look to the future when it comes to technology. One key way to encourage success is by motivating your salespeople to keep an eye on the market for any tools that might help them sell smarter in the future.

Think of it like this. the more tools your sales team are comfortable with using, the more ways they are able to wow and assist new customers, providing a level of insight not available elsewhere. This can so often be the difference between winning new business and not.

CHAPTER THREE

High Performance Teams Remote Workplace

High Performance Teams (Remote Workforce) are organizations, teams or groups working in a virtual environment that are focused on achieving the same goals. Bringing team members together through a virtual environment can be a challenge task. This course identifies these challenges and helps you to push through to success. With our High Performance Teams (Remote Workforce) course, you will begin to see how important it is to develop a core set of high performance skills, while working remotely. By knowing and managing the way people interact in a remote environment, you will be setting up your high performance teams to accomplish any task.

The popularity of remote work is rising fast. Multiple research studies show that employees who are able to skip commuting and work away from the office, whether at home, a coffee shop or somewhere in between, are happier, more productive and less likely to jump ship. But overseeing a team of remote employees doesn't come naturally to many managers, who are accustomed to seeing their employees in the office at least a few days each week. Some even question how they can know if people working away from the office are really working. The first thing we teach leaders in that situation is management by objectives—how you can give people the benefit of the doubt by setting expectations upfront and having a clear understanding of roles and responsibilities and timelines.

Managing Accountability: Proponents of remote work see it as a viable way for companies to expand and diversify their talent pool, reduce overhead expenses, and respond to business demands in real time. Yet many remote teams fail to meet their objectives. The guiding principles of leadership are the same regardless of whether the team is located under one roof or geographically dispersed.

Overcoming Virtual Distance: Digital communication enables remote work, but it creates a whole set of new problems. It's easy to forget that you're dealing with real people. Virtual distance, is a sense of emotional and psychological detachment that builds up over time when people become over-reliant on technology to mediate their relationships. When virtual teams underperform, companies often think that geographic issues are the main problem and gravitate toward strategies to fix that problem the root cause is virtual distance. It changes the way that people relate to each other. The greater the virtual distance, the higher the negative impact on the team in terms of innovation effectiveness, trust, work satisfaction, role and goal clarity, and project success. Team leaders can reduce virtual distance by creating an environment where team members feel emotionally and psychologically connected to one another and to the business. Employee volunteering is another effective way to boost engagement and morale. Remote teams can identify causes they care about and how they want to participate. They can conduct virtual charity auctions or fundraise among themselves for events in the community, such as food drives or charity walks/runs.

Have a remote work policy: Successful companies have introduced or updated their remote work policy to keep the workforce informed and empowered. Your remote work policy should clearly define the team's scheduled meetings, operational guidelines and expectations to take away as many of the unknowns as possible. This may also include organizational charts, an outline of performance expectations, an equipment checklist, performance tools, available cultural development resources to avoid any sort of remote work isolation, and burnout prevention tips. A remote work policy will enable the teams to remain disciplined even if they are working from the comfort of their homes. It will keep your employees happy, content, and healthy, while making them more productive.

Train your team on remote work skills: Training and development are crucial in sustaining a self-managed and empowered workforce. Make sure you have training programs for both new hires as well as existing staff to develop a learning attitude within them. The programs may include soft skills required for remote work or an introduction to remote work tools such as video conferencing tools like Zoom, collaboration apps like Asana and Microsoft Teams, and more. Since communication will be held online, teaching soft skills like video call etiquette, communication skills, etc., is also essential. The goal is to commit your team to long-term learning.

Engage and communicate: Working remotely means your team is at a high risk of experiencing isolation. Remote work also brings many communications challenges. As a rule of thumbs, leaders should:

- Over-communicate rather than under-communicate
- Communicate via phone call and video call when written communication gets confusing
- Check in with your team individually to determine whether they need any support
- Get to know how the teams are doing and feeling with their responsibilities and deliverables
- Encourage your employees to share their views, opinions and ideas
- Give your staff the freedom to collaborate to solve problems without you

Make sure you set a foundation of psychological safety and trust that is characterized by mutual respect and open communication as well as ensure your team has all the right tools and resources to succeed in their roles. In addition, being explicit in your work policy helps your remote team understand the expectations and boundaries from the get-go. Lastly, establish regular rituals such as weekly group meetings and regular one-on-one catchups with your direct reports allowing everyone to stay aligned on priorities while strengthening personal relationships within your team.

CHAPTER FOUR

In Person Sales

In-person sales are the first step in running a profitable business—and it's a step you can't afford to skip. Typically, clients make purchase decisions out of emotion. Ideally, you want them to see their images for the first time in person, with you. In-person sales have a variety of benefits that will allow you to increase your overall income as you appeal to customers' senses and emotions to encourage them to make purchase decisions.

Time consideration: In person sales can be a LOT of work, but you'll most likely have fewer clients since you're talking about a higher-end market. You'll likely have to schedule a lot of meetings with clients, say at coffee shops or the like. As you can guess, this service is HIGHLY customized, meaning you are spending more time with each client. The time it takes to research product pricing and your cost of doing business. This can take a TON of time. You have to be very detailed in your costs to make sure that you are profitable. You're going to be spending a lot of time with your clients. This includes your initial meeting, the actual presentation session, in-person sale meeting and ordering, overall correspondence time, travel time to meetings, and creating and delivering the final product.

Build a Connection: When clients view their images for the first time, they'll have an emotional reaction to those images. Putting up an online gallery allows customers to visit the images several times, gradually reducing the emotional impact. The more times they look, the more the emotional impact will lessen, and the less attached to those images your customers will be. In some cases, you may leave hundreds and even thousands of dollars on the table simply by allowing customers to view their images at their leisure.

Appeal to the Senses: An appeal to the senses is great for your sales strategy—especially when you're working with women. Using a beautiful, high-end album that your clients can hold in their lap is a great way to connect with them. Women, in particular, like to run their hands over the leather and feel the weight of the album. Online product galleries reduce this incredible opportunity.

Connect Personally With Clients: As you visit with your clients, you're also getting to know them. You're coming into their home, taking a look at their style, and giving them a firsthand look at the images that will look best on their walls. With the right presentation, you can even give clients a look at exactly your product is.

Throughout your conversations with the prospect, you can consider recommending other products and services that could help your prospect, outside of the pain-point your own product solves. This should come up naturally, but it shows that you're trying to provide value and not just selling your product.

Setting Your Sales Approach Apart: In general, the steps in your sales process will help you prospect with greater efficiency, initiate contact, get to know the prospect's needs and desires in greater detail, and convince qualified prospects that what you sell is the best option for addressing their points of concern. At each stage, however, you need to be able to do two things: Differentiate yourself from your competition, and establish your credibility. If you can't do this at every stage of the process, your prospects won't give you the time of day. They need to be confident in you as a salesperson, and that can be addressed through the things you say (both in person and online) and other visible markers of credibility.

Internet Marketing Fundamentals

Internet marketing has become one of the most trending terms recently. Every kind of business is adopting digital marketing techniques. Consider a large or small business, everyone has adopted digital marketing activities in some capacity or other. In this article, we would cover what digital marketing is, its importance, and the fundamentals of digital marketing also referred to as the types of digital marketing.

Internet marketing is marketing your product, whether a good or service, through digital means. It involves marketing through online mediums and can be understood as the opposite of traditional marketing. Internet marketing constitutes all the modern marketing techniques and is a growing marketing trend, which is why it is important to learn about the fundamentals of digital marketing. It has opened many avenues for different organizations, and every brand has to imperatively employ digital marketing techniques for leading their business successfully,

Why Internet or digital marketing is important: The number of social media users is equivalent to 32.3% approximately of the total population. Now, if we consider this number, then we would easily get the answer to the question of why digital marketing is important. When 32.3% of the population is on social media, then it is only smart to use that medium for your benefit. There are many reasons why digital marketing has been booming.

1. **Wider audience-** With traditional methods of marketing, your efforts get limited to a particular demographic but with digital marketing, your presence can be felt globally, hence reaching a wider audience.

1. **Compete with the big forces**- Now the marketing opportunities are not limited to big businesses alone, but anyone can use digital marketing methods for their benefit, hence placing a small brand also in the major leagues.

3. **Reach to potential customers**- Earlier it was difficult to reach out to potential customers, but with the efforts of digital marketing it has become easy to identify and reach the target audience. Targeting the potential audience will yield better results.

4. **Track the reach**- Traditional marketing methods were hard to track. It is difficult to track how many people saw a particular billboard and ultimately made the purchase, but with digital marketing, it is possible with various tools that help to track the social media presence, website activity, etc.

5. **Return on Investment**- Email marketing ROI stands at 42x. For every rupee brands invest in email marketing, they receive 42 paisa in return. This is the kind of return we are talking about. It is huge and hence it would be a great decision to invest in digital marketing opportunities and see your business grow.

Fundamentals of Digital Marketing

SEO Search Engine Optimization: The first and the most inexpensive part of the fundamentals of digital marketing is SEO which stands for Search Engine Optimization. It is one of the best and simplest ways to increase a brand's visibility. SEO can be explained as the process of optimizing the content through the strategic use of keywords and complying with the algorithm of search engines so that during a search on Google, Bing, Yahoo, or any other search engine, they index the content and show it to the right people. The more visibility one can get through a search, the more are the chances of attracting traffic and potential consumers. This explains why understanding SEO is important. The Internet has become the top medium for people to get information, so if businesses want to get noticed and get ranked on a search, they have to invest in SEO activities. SEO is the organic way of gaining traffic. It is through the bots that Google or any other search engine uses that indexes the content. The bots crawl the web, and using various algorithms, they analyze the content index and then decide in which order the content would appear in the search results.

Online Advertising: Where SEO was referred to as the inexpensive aspect of the fundamentals of digital marketing, online advertising is the paid aspect, also termed as paid media. When you search on Google, let's say free courses with certificates, on the top of the search results, you would notice some links before which the word, Ad is mentioned. This is an example of online advertising. All those ads that pop up on your screen while you are scrolling through Facebook or Instagram are also examples of paid media. There are many channels for online advertising like Youtube ads, Facebook ads, LinkedIn ads, Instagram ads, Google ads, PPC Campaigns, etc. Brands have to identify what works best for them and which channel would be the best way to reach their target audience. Online advertising is considered the best way to reach the target audience and increase brand awareness. The mediums like Google and Facebook have provided many resources that help the brand in building their ads and reaching the targeted audience. Also, online advertising has offered the brands the ability to keep track and analyze the reach, which is not possible with traditional marketing.

Content Marketing: To put it simply, content marketing is a strategy to target the desired audience by creating relevant content, which can be in the form of articles, videos, podcasts, or any other media meant to engage and retain an audience. It can be achieved through blogs, newsletters, emails, etc. Content marketing is also an organic way of increasing traffic by developing SEO- friendly content and helping in increasing brand awareness. Content marketing, when done strategically, leads to great results, which can be analyzed through the fact that businesses with blogs get 67% more leads than other companies. Content marketing helps in earning leads and helps brands to convey the product ideas and vision.

Email Marketing: Email marketing is an easy and effective way to stay connected with existing and potential customers. Email marketing is nothing but generic mail that is used to target the audience. It can be understood as an advertisement that is aimed at garnering traffic on the website and has the highest conversion rates. Most of the email marketing constitutes emails that communicate new offers and coupons to spike the recipient's interest.

Social Media Marketing: Using social media platforms to market a product or a service is social media marketing. It is the easiest and most effective way to connect with the target audience. We all have witnessed the power that social media holds. The impact of social media on our opinions is immense. There are millions of people on social media swaying others with their opinions, and if brands use this fact for their benefit, then that becomes social media marketing. Also, in comparison to the before-mentioned fundamentals, social media marketing can be adopted by any brand size, small or big. If you are running a business in 2021, then make sure that your presence is felt on social media. Every brand should aim to stay relevant on social media and be equipped with the knowledge of current trends. Social media marketing also allows the brands the opportunity to track the reach of their content, and with the various tools that are offered by the social media platforms themselves, it has become very easy for the brands to identify patterns and find what works best for them and where they can improve.

Pay-Per-Click: Pay-per-click is a part of paid media that is used to increase the rankings on search engines through paid means. Pay-per-click is used to improve rankings by moving on top of the search results and drive more traffic. The advertisement stays for as long it is being paid for, afterward, it won't exist. It is called PPC, as every time the advertisement is clicked by anyone, your ad account is charged for it. PPC is a short-term solution to drive traffic, and many big companies invest heavily in it during seasonal deals, new product introductions, etc. The amount charged is fixed on the basis of the time period of the ad, the keywords used (more competitive the keywords, more would be the price).

Affiliate/Influencer Marketing: Affiliate marketing is getting the product promoted through another person and paying commission to them on every sale made. It is using the reach of an individual to your own advantage. Here, the affiliate needs not to be an individual alone but can be an entity also. The affiliate promotes the product, whether a good or service, through any medium like a Youtube video or a blog, and when anyone clicks on the link provided to them for the product, ultimately buying it, then they are compensated for it through commission. Most of the companies have started collaborating with influencers to increase their brand awareness. Social media influencers have a great impact on the views of their fan base, and brands are using this to their advantage by getting their products advertised through influencers. It benefits both the parties as influencers who here are working as affiliates get the commission as an incentive, and the brands get the sales.

• 21 •

CHAPTER SIX

Marketing Basics

Marketing concepts or marketing management philosophies refer to the philosophies utilized by the businesses to direct their marketing efforts. Mainly, marketing concepts denote the philosophies a business uses to define and accomplish the needs of its customers, serving both the consumer and the company. The same philosophy cannot be helpful for all types of businesses. So, different types of businesses use different marketing management philosophies or marketing concepts. Marketing management is a process of controlling the marketing aspects, setting the goals of a company, organizing the plans step by step, taking decisions for the firm, and executing them to get the maximum turn over by meeting the consumers' demands.

A person who is a marketing manager must do a deep study to have the idea of actually what is marketing management and how to make it better in your firm's favor. Marketing management is based on product, place, price, and promotion to attract consumers.

Marketing Management is Important Because

Marketing management is of importance as it helps to stand competent in highly thriving competition in the market. This also helps to develop strategies to improve profits and reduce the cost of products. Marketing management has become the major source of exchange and transfer of goods.

Helps to maintain the company's reputation: A good company is recognized by its reputation in the market. The marketing includes selling, buying, exchanging, transporting goods which build its reputation. If a company falls well on these parameters, it stands firm and gains a clear and good reputation among the public which is the sole of a business and cannot be denied. If a good reputation is built, it will be beneficial for the company for its growth and promotion. When it comes to reputation, good and reputable companies do not compromise for this at all and try. Companies with a good reputation get more opportunities to grow and get more tenders to make them market competent and economically strong.

Helps to boost the economy of the company: Marketing management decides the ways to beat the market competition and make good sales. They develop plans to advertise their products in an affected way and when the products are advertised, they are on the radar to be viewed and known by the public. Advertisements help to spread the product description to a great level through friends and family. Suppose when a girl came to know about the flat 50 percent sale on the clothing brands she will tell her friends and family, spreading the advertisement of that brand's products lively.

Promotes the new ideas: The marketing management helps to promote new ideas which are depending upon the benefits and offers for the public to be grabbed quickly. These ideas keep nourishing and diversifying the companies by keeping them distinctive from other companies' presence in the market. These ideas are useful for the company to know the demand of today's market and do not let it lead in the wrong direction.

Source of advertising the new products: Newly launched products by a company with which the public is not familiar, need to be advertised. Marketing management allows the product advertisement in a better and effective way that could grab a great crowd of public towards the new product.

Production Concept: This concept is based on an idea that inexpensive and widely available products generate more sales because customers prefer those. This is quite similar to the Say's Law which states 'Supply creates its own demand'. So, companies produce the product on a large scale and make sure that it is easily available everywhere to the customer. The large scale of production of the product helps the companies to avail the economies of scale which lead to inexpensive products and thus attracting more customers. The drawback of this concept is that it focuses only on production but not on the product quality which in the long run may cause decreased sales if the product is not up to the mark. This philosophy is only applicable when the demand exceeds the supply. Again, a customer is not always attracted to an inexpensive product because his/ her purchase decision may be influenced by other factors. The drawback of this concept is that it focuses only on production but not on the product quality which in the long run may cause decreased sales if the product is not up to the mark. This philosophy is only applicable when the demand exceeds the supply.

Again, a customer is not always attracted to an inexpensive product because his/ her purchase decision may be influenced by other factors.

Objectives of marketing management: The objectives of each business are pre-set which is led by objectives of marketing management. The basic and important objectives of marketing management are:

Attracting new customers: The important objective of marketing management is to attract new customers to increase the sales of products. Different strategies are set to make sure that maximum customers get attracted to the company's products like displaying ads on TV channels or social media, pamphlets, and arranging a sales team that demonstrates the products.

Satisfying the demands of customers: Another important objective of marketing management is to keep satisfied the customer who is associated with the company's products for a long period. For this purpose, the quality matters a lot but apart from this good service is also concerned like an on-time supply of products and without damage, the products are supplied.

Profitability: Without earning profit a company could not survive longer. Earning profit is the backbone of a company. It is necessary to earn profit for growing, diversifying a business, and its maintenance as well. For this purpose, a company must know what is market management? And how to achieve these market targets? A company's management team keeps the marketing on track by entertaining their old and reliable customers and attracting the new customer to make maximum profit for maximum growth.

Maximizing the market share: Another objective of marketing management is to make maximum marketing share. For this purpose, companies use different tools to get maximum market sales of their products by having comparison with a market economy. Sometimes, companies offer discounts to attract customers. Sometimes, they do attractive and unique packaging and offer promotions.

Creating a good public reputation: Public reputation plays an important role in the growth of a company. If the company has stood as a good public figure it means it has more chances to grow and diversify but if stands with a bad reputation, it will no longer survive

Process of marketing management: This is very obvious to know about what marketing management is on today's demand and how we can achieve it. Every company has its specific objectives and goals that make it distinctive from other companies in the market. But some steps needed to make your marketing management effective are enlisted below:

Define your mission statement and work for it: Mission statements should be set before doing anything. The company's marketing management and stakeholder should decide on a very effective and strong mission statement. After that, they should map out their company's goals and objectives which can be taken for a long time. The mission statement should be very clear and transparent to others and have the potential to attract customers. The goals a company has to set should be unique, aspiring, based on reality, and for a specific time.

Analysis of industrial rank of your business: Competition among the companies has arisen to the highest peak in marketing. Different companies are marketing their company's products in different but unique ways that aid them to maintain their position in this competitive environment. A company needs to know what its position in the market is alarming or satisfying for its survival and growth. For this purpose, the company has to analyze its rank and its sustainability after each short period of time. Marketing management should analyze the strong and weak aspects of the company and should work hard to overcome the weak aspects by shifting their paradigms that may cover the weaknesses. Other important factors are trending and threatening; trending provides opportunities to do the things which are on-demand in the market and these are beneficial for the business but the threatening is totally opposite to it. With the obstacles an old business may get from the newly rising businesses that stand against this company including different issues like politics or economic hurdles. It is a matter of great concern that how can you keep your customers engaged and how can you accept and reflect the change in your company's marketing style to get maximum growth.

Processing towards work: Now it is time to execute the planning you have made with your managerial team for the marketing of your company's products. Different campaigns are run and the wordy plan is executed as action.

Keep evaluating, modifying, and repeating the strategies: After that when you have executed the plan to get fruitful results, it is time to evaluate your company's outcomes and modify them if there is a requirement but if they are going well and result-oriented, they are repeated.

Functions of marketing management: A company performs different tasks when it actually knows what is marketing management, has developed a plan to achieve its goals, and prepared the track to take follow-up of output and position in the market. Some of the functions and tasks of marketing management are enlisted below:

Development of products: Marketing management stays up to date and evaluates the reviews of the products launched in the market. They work for the development of products by taking into account the raw materials, technologies, and good innovations that they could get good reviews and popularity in public. Products are passed through different processes to make sure that they are able to be delivered to the market for customer use.

Promotions are made: The products of a company cannot be sold without being easily available and advertised. Marketing management makes sure that either their products are known by the public. They use different social media platforms like Facebook, Instagram, Whatsapp, Pinterest, Twitter, etc. to make their product ready for promotion. Most people use these social media apps and see different advertisements. If these advertisements are developed in an effective way they can be captured by a maximum number of eyes and ordered for use.

Selling Concept: Selling Concept is only concerned with selling the product whatever may be the quality of the product and need of the customer. The chief motive is making money, not developing a relationship with the customers. So, there is less possibility of repeated sales. Companies applying this philosophy can even deceive the customers to sell their products. The drawback of this concept is that it lacks foresightedness because the companies focus on selling what they produce instead of focusing on the need of the market.

Marketing Concept: A company following selling concept cannot have long-term existence in the market because it cannot fulfill customers' needs. Companies have to make products fulfilling their customers' needs to be successful in today's era. So, the marketing concept came into existence. This concept is based on an idea that customers buy the products accomplishing their needs. Companies based on marketing philosophy perform customer-researches to know their needs and wants and make products to meet the same better than their competing companies. In this way, the company builds a customer relationship, becomes profitable and earns goodwill. But still, many companies follow other philosophies and generate profits. The choice of the concept is totally dependent on the demand, supply, and the engaged parties' needs.

Societal Marketing Concept: The societal marketing concept is based on the marketing concept just adding the philosophy of social welfare with it. Companies concentrate on fulfilling their customers' needs as well as contributing to social welfare without polluting or affecting the environment and natural resources. According to this concept, company or business being a part of the society has *corporate social responsibilities* such as eliminating illiteracy, poverty, controlling alarming population growth, ensuring better health and treatment facilities, helping victims of different natural calamities like flood, cyclone, excess cold, draught, etc.

Holistic Marketing Concept: The holistic marketing concept is newly added to the existing marketing management concepts. According to this concept, a business and its different parts are one single entity and have a common goal, aligned and integrated activities to achieve that goal. This concept focuses on meeting customer needs in a better and consistent way as well as performing the social responsibilities. The holistic marketing concept is very important for brand building, consistency, efficiency, and effectiveness.

Applicability of this Concept: Many big reputed companies like banks, TV channels, telecommunication companies, etc. are now applying this concept. Business people should have a clear and complete idea about the basic concepts of Marketing Management to achieve long-term success.

CHAPTER SEVEN

Media and Public Relations

The idea of public relations as a strategic function is lost on those who adhere to the common misconception of PR as nothing more than "spin" or "free publicity" through news coverage. When they hear the term "public relations," they think of technical aspects such as writing press releases or organizing press conferences. Organizational leaders who desire to excel would be well served to incorporate a broader view of public relations into their leadership philosophies. At its heart, public relations is about **relationships**. Publics are stakeholders, those groups of people whose opinions may have an impact on an organization's ability to achieve its goals. If an organization is to build mutually beneficial relationships with its key publics, it must understand what matters to them. The organization's leaders must know who their critical publics are and what makes them tick. Additionally, organizational leaders must understand the communication environment within which they are attempting to relate to their publics. This involves monitoring the environment to gain understanding of public opinion and current issues that have the potential to impact the organization's activities. This is easier said than done.

Leaders who have effectively incorporated public relations into their management philosophy pro-actively consider questions such as these. Public relations is a strategic function of leadership. A thorough, research-based understanding of your publics and the communication environment in which you operate will strengthen your ability to build relationships and communicate with those publics. This will increase your capacity to achieve your organizational goals.

Positive: Pessimists don't change the world. It's always the optimists, believers, and dreamers we see changing the world. Teams and clients need to be inspired and energized and that requires a leader with a positive outlook on life and for the company. If a company wants results, there's no room for a pessimistic leader.

Being invisible: A strong PR leader isn't interested in being famous—they're committed to connecting organizations to stakeholders. A strong PR leader's work might place a client in the spotlight, but that's the client's glory. PR leaders don't have time to worry about getting themselves into the spotlight. Their only concern is using media to their clients' advantage and achieving their clients' goals.

Continually develop leadership skills: Leadership skills are acquired over time through training and experience. There isn't a single leadership course in existence that can produce leaders who won't benefit from continued growth. Developing leadership in any industry is a continual process. Effective PR leaders are constantly seeking opportunities to grow and develop their skills. Seminars, workshops, and other resources are always on their schedule. For instance, their blogs dissolve the notion that leadership is about being the best and emphasize the importance of promoting psychological safety in teams—two important and often overlooked aspects of leadership.

Share your vision: You can't keep your vision to yourself. Being a leader requires getting people to follow you without questions or doubt. You have to share your vision to get people on board with what you're asking them to do. When a team knows what's expected and knows where the leader is taking them, they're confident in their ability to do their job and are more likely to trust their leader.

How Each Practice Is Valuable for Creating a Powerhouse Strategy

We know that earned and owned media make a great pair. But how do content marketing, thought leadership, and PR meld to make one heck of a strategy?

Content Marketing: Content marketing is the overarching practice that drives your efforts, whether you're using earned media, owned media, or (ideally) some combination. They're both vital to growing your sales pipeline and converting leads into clients. A content marketing strategy helps you use both types to accomplish those goals effectively.

Content marketing can take several forms: guest content that you contribute to online publications; written, visual, or interactive blog content; email; PR opportunities; and social media posts, to name a few. Your content marketing strategy should include a variety of those forms.

Thought Leadership: Ah, thought leadership — love this term or hate it, it's not going anywhere. Thought leadership falls under the content marketing umbrella because that's how subject matter experts often build their influence: through content. The difference is that this type of content isn't necessarily tied to the part of your content marketing strategy that promotes your company or directly addresses a prospect's objections to working with you.

Thought leadership is focused on an individual within your company and his or her experiences, expertise, and insight. It's just as important as the blog posts, videos, and social content you publish because it shows that you are the expert and that real humans exist behind your brand. People want to work with (and buy from) the best in the industry; thought leadership content shows them that "best in the industry" means you.

Public Relations: PR is an effective form of earned media because when someone else sings your praises or covers what your company is up to, you gain instant credibility. We're a content marketing company, and we can't deny how powerful PR and press mentions are. When an influencer writes about Influence & Co., we see our traffic increase, and we often use it as sales enablement copy. Plus, it's awesome to see that stamp of approval for all the work we do. But because we're also using a content marketing strategy, we can better leverage those PR opportunities. If we were to use only that PR and forget the content on our site and our guest content, how would we back up the praises that influencer sang in his press mention? And vice versa: If we'd neglected the content on our site and never guest-contributed a single thought leadership article, the chances of our being mentioned in the first place would have been a lot smaller. That's why they all need to work together.

Practice What You Preach: One of Influence & Co.'s top online lead sources is an article in Inc. that mentions us as one of six content marketing companies dominating the industry. It was such an honor to be included on that list, and it has served us well as a great jumping-off point for marketing professionals who are scouring Google for companies to vet. Because that article links to our site, readers have the chance to look around and see what we're about — and because we've invested in content there, we're able to receive contact forms and get people on the phone with us. Readers who enjoy that content continue to read his posts, follow him on social media, and visit our website. There, they can check out our blog, download gated content, subscribe to our email lists, and more so that we can continue delivering valuable content to them and nurture them to a sale.

See how nicely everything comes together? : This is how we integrate PR and thought leadership into our content strategy, and it's how we help our clients, too — whether they're working with a PR firm already or they're using our PR partnership services. So the next time you're wondering why you need thought leadership content if you're using PR or you're struggling to explain to your team how these practices work together, remember "Jerry Maguire." Content marketing, thought leadership, and PR complete one another — you've just got to have the strategy to make it work.

Effective PR leaders focus on clarity: Conflicts are inevitable, and clarity is always the answer. Effective PR leaders are willing to repeat themselves for clarification without getting frustrated. People need leaders who keep them on track and continually guide them toward the overall goal. People need frequent reassurance, even if it means repeating what was said last week.

Strong PR leaders are decisive in good and bad times: A leader who can't make up his or her mind will lose their team's confidence. A strong PR leader will be decisive regardless of what's going on. For example, when team members aren't in agreement, a strong PR leader will listen to everyone's point of view and make the tough decisions necessary to move forward.

Strong PR leaders focus on developing trust: PR leaders need to focus on developing and maintaining trust with their team. Without trust, people might abandon the team when disagreements arise. Leaders who exhibit behavior like belittling others and having explosive outbursts will never earn their team's trust. These leaders are considered toxic and are cited as the reason 73 percent of people intend to leave the company they work for.

Public Relations Roles: In general, public relations professionals can be communication managers who organize and integrate communication activities, or they can be communication technicians who primarily write and construct messages. Research in this area led to the identification of four specific roles: the technician role and three types of communication managers. Most practitioners begin their careers as communication technicians. This role requires executing strategies with the communication tactics of news releases, employee newsletters, position papers, media placements, Web site content, speeches, blogs, and social media messaging. Practitioners in this role are usually not involved in defining problems and developing solutions, but base their tactics on the technical skill of writing. The expert prescriber is similar to the role a doctor performs with a patient:

He or she is an authority on a particular industry, problem, or type of public relations and is given the primary responsibility to handle this function as a consultant or with little input or participation by other senior management. The communication facilitator is a boundary spanner who listens to and brokers information between the organization and its key publics. The goal of this role is to provide both management and publics the information they need for making decisions of mutual interest. The problem-solving facilitator collaborates with other managers to define and solve problems. This role requires that the professional is a part of the dominant coalition of the organization and has access to other senior managers. The problem-solving facilitator helps other managers think through organizational problems using a public relations perspective.

The communication manager is involved in the strategic thinking of an organization and must be able to conduct research and measurement and share data that informs better decisions for managing relationships with key publics. The communications manager thinks strategically, which means he or she will be focused on the efforts of the organization that contribute to the mutually beneficial relationships that help an organization achieve its bottom-line goals. These efforts are not limited to communication strategies, but include monitoring an organization's external environment, scanning for issues that might impact the organization, and helping an organization adapt to the needs of its stakeholders. A study on excellence in the practice of public relations found that one of the major predictors of excellence was whether the role of the top public relations executive was a manager role or a technician role. Those in the management role were much more likely to have a positive impact on the organization's public relations practice. In order for corporate communication to function strategically, the executive in charge of the function must have a place at the decision-making table.

The C-Suite: Virtually all organizations are run by a senior leadership team that is responsible for setting strategy and carrying out the organization's vision. Although publicly traded companies, as well as nonprofit organizations, may be governed ultimately by a board of directors, this board looks to the chief executive and his or her senior team to operate the company on a day-to-day basis.

The key functions in an organization include finance, headed by a chief financial officer (CFO); legal, which reports to the General Counsel; human resources, led by a chief personnel officer (CPO); information services, reporting to the chief information officer (CIO); marketing, often led by a chief marketing officer (CMO); and communication, which reports to the chief communications officer (CCO). These functional areas serve the operations of the company, which in some cases report to a president or chief operating officer. In many cases the CEO also is president/COO (chief operating officer) of the organization. Although organizational structures vary from company to company, these basic functional areas are usually present in the senior team. In some cases, the communication function is subordinated under another area, such as marketing, legal, or human resources. When this is the case, it becomes more difficult for the senior communications leader to play a meaningful role in the strategic decision-making process. The communication function brings to the senior team a different perspective from these other areas. The legal function is focused primarily on compliance with the law; marketing is focused primarily on the company's competitive position with the customer; human resources (HR) is focused almost exclusively on employee compensation and development issues. In other words, communication is the only function with eyes on *all* the publics inside and outside of the organization, and should be included in strategic decision making.

Role of Communication in Decision Making: One of the common denominators for officers in the C-suite is the imperative to make good decisions that affect their ability to positively contribute to the goals of the organization. The ability to make good decisions often defines a valuable manager. To make good decisions, managers need good information. By definition, good information helps reduce uncertainty in making a decision. Rarely is a decision made with utter certainty, but managers need enough information to have confidence that their decisions will result in positive consequences. This information is provided as data regarding these various functions: product testing, market research, legal precedents, and financial statements. Since public relations' role is to help the organization develop and maintain good relationships, it must provide data or information about how the organization can achieve this. This is how strategic public relations earns its seat at the executive table. The communication function looks at all the stakeholders in the organization and uses a variety of tools and tactics to enhance relationships with these publics. At its best, the communication function uses research and monitoring methods to keep a finger on the pulse of internal and external perceptions of the organization. It uses a variety of communication channels to enhance the organization's reputation. And most importantly it provides strategic counsel to the organization's leaders to help the team make better decisions. Some have suggested that the communication function serves or should serve as the corporate conscience. They contend that communication leaders have a uniquely objective perspective that allows them to weigh the sometimes conflicting needs of different publics and to help the organization make more balanced decisions. Although there is much truth to this perspective, we add that the conscience of the organization, its moral obligation to do the right thing, is one that is shared by all who lead it, including the CEO, the board, and the senior management team.

As the top communication professional, the CCO has an important responsibility to ensure that all key stakeholders are given due consideration when critical decisions are made. In that regard, the CCO acts as the voice for many who are not in the room when choices are made. He or she must keep in mind the minority shareholders, overlooked employee segments, nongovernmental organizations, special interest groups, elected officials, community leaders, and others who may be affected by the decision and who have influential roles in their respective areas. By providing this overarching perspective, the CCO does much more than deliver tactical communication products. This strategic counsel is what CEOs and other leaders are increasingly seeking in all members of the senior team. By delivering it, the CCO enhances the value of the function and ensures ongoing participation in charting the future course for the company.

Strategy and Profit Motivation: Public relations as a profession is often thought of as nothing more than a simple set of tactics. Far too often those in the profession are portrayed in the media and in popular culture as a group of empty-headed party planners or deceptive flacks willing to say anything to get publicity for their clients. The tools of the trade—news releases, press conferences, media events, employee newsletters—are considered as discrete tactics that rarely if ever are driven by an underlying strategy. This, like other stereotypes, is simply not supported by fact. As practiced by most large organizations and agencies, public relations is an integral part of overall strategy. Communication programs are developed based on extensive research to address specific business objectives with stated outcomes, target audiences, and key messages. The results of these efforts can be measured, both qualitatively and quantitatively. Think of it this way: When an organization develops a strategic plan, it usually does so with a relatively small number of key executives. These leaders look at the company's strengths, organization, challenging issues, and potential problems that could arise. They consider the organization's financial position, its growth prospects, its competitive position, and the changing landscape in which it operates.

When they have considered all of these factors, they map out a strategy that will build on the company's current strengths, address its relative areas of weakness, take advantage of opportunities, and prepare for looming threats. They may decide, for example, to be the low-cost provider in their industry segment. Or they may decide to take advantage of their expertise in new product development, or to exploit their superior distribution network. At some point, the strategy must be executed by a much larger, geographically dispersed network of employees. This is where the communication strategy becomes crucial. If a company has a long track record of fighting with its employees over issues like pay, benefits, union representation, child care programs, or workplace safety, it will be much more difficult to call upon them to launch a new initiative aimed at improving customer service.

In large measure, an important role of the communication function team is to help balance the needs of all publics—employees, investors, customers, communities—as the organization makes key decisions. For example, assume that a company is facing financial difficulties due to declining market share. They are faced with the decision of closing a Units since that level of manufacturing capacity is no longer needed. In the past, they simply might have turned to the public relations executive and said, we're closing the ABC Unit. Try to put a good face on it. An organization that views the communication function as a strategic partner instead would say, We've got too much manufacturing capacity; operations is recommending that we close ABC. We'd like you to take a look at the impact this will have with our employees, customers, and the community there and help us measure this as we examine the alternatives. There may be another choice that won't be as painful to the organization.

Balancing the needs of publics is just one facet of the impact public relations can have on achieving organizational goals. It obviously depends on the organization, but in almost every case, effective communication programs help drive strategy from conception to delivery. Successful internal communication programs can improve the ability of supervisors to motivate employees and build pride in the organization. Creative external communication programs can improve customer relationships, build brand recognition, encourage investor interest in a publicly traded company, and increase the effectiveness of traditional advertising and marketing efforts. Community outreach programs can help local residents appreciate the impact of a company on the surrounding area in which it operates. The impact of well-conceived strategic communication programs can be profound, and many companies have already benefited by recognizing this importance and building upon the strengths public relations brings to the table. The communication executive does not own these responsibilities alone. They are shared with other members of the leadership team. But the communication executive can and should take a lead role in ensuring that these responsibilities are fulfilled by the organization.

CHAPTER EIGHT

Motivating your sales team

Ironically enough, many incentive plans come close to ignoring core performers. Why does this group tend to be off the radar screen? One reason is that sales managers don't identify with them. At many companies the managers are former rainmakers, so they pay the current rainmakers an undue amount of attention. As a consequence, core performers are often passed over for promotion and neglected at annual sales meetings. But this is not in the best interest of the company. Core performers usually represent the largest part of the sales force, and companies cannot make their numbers if they're not in the game. Here are some proven strategies for keeping them there. Improving your team's skill set is a largely objective process. By evaluating current performance metrics and comparing them to a successful end state, you can diagnose what areas need improvement and act accordingly. But motivation is far harder. Not only are there are many external factors that affect motivation, every person requires different incentives and motivational tactics. In my decades as a sales leader, I've used the following strategies to successfully motivate my team and drive motivation through the roof.

Build trust with the people on your team: The foundation of motivation is trust. If your team doesn't trust you and doesn't believe you have their best interests at heart, it'll be difficult for them to feel inspired and driven by their work. When salespeople are unmotivated, you won't be able to re-inspire them unless you have an open and honest conversation about their challenges and goals something that simply won't happen without trust. It's a vicious or virtuous cycle. Managers have to create trust and then maintain it by engaging with their team in a consistent, nurturing fashion. The best way to build trust is to be completely transparent. Simply discussing trust can be a great way of starting off on the right foot. It's pretty direct and it's a great way to explain to the team that I am interested in working on a business relationship, rather than being their boss.

Ask your direct reports how they like to be managed.

Three important things:

1. Everybody's personality is different.
2. I want to be an effective manager for your work style and personality.
3. I can modify my behavior to fit your needs. How do you want to be managed?

Just as different prospects will require different selling styles and effective salespeople understand how to adapt to those styles, effective managers understand that the best way to get results out of their team is to fit into their reports' worlds, instead of forcing one method of communication or strategy on everyone else. Here are some questions I ask my direct reports to help them figure out what their work style is like:

1. What is the pace of interaction that you prefer? Do you want to meet with me once a week, every other week, or multiple times a week?
2. How do you want me to give you feedback?
3. Do you prefer public or private praise and feedback?
4. What type of feedback do you prefer?
5. If I hear something amiss, do you want me to tell you, email you, wait until our one-on-one, or something else?
6. If something I do gets on your nerves, will you let me know?

Understand your direct reports' personal and professional goals: You can't motivate someone unless you know what drives them. Understand what your direct reports each want to accomplish in their personal and professional lives. This will not only show you the type of person they are, but also give your insight into what things will motivate them the most.

Once you understand their goals, ask them the following questions:

1. *Are you motivated right now?*
2. *What motivates you long term?*
3. *What can you do to motivate yourself?*
4. *How will I know if you are not motivated?*
5. *What do you want me to do if you don't appear motivated?*

Even if it seems obvious, you always need to ask. If they can't tell you the answers to these questions, give those 48 hours to figure it out. Forcing your reps to be self-reflective makes it more likely they'll give you thoughtful answers, which will be better for you both in the long run.

Set daily, weekly, and monthly goals: Different salespeople are motivated in different ways. Some people are motivated by team-wide sales contests. Some are driven by quota achievement. Some are motivated by qualitative improvements. Some people are motivated by their impact on the organization. Some people are motivated by money.

Here's how you should think about each type of goal and SPIF (sales performance incentive fund):

- Daily: This is a very short-term goal designed to break a rep out of their funk. The SPIF should be something fun but lightweight, since the rep isn't doing that much to earn it.
- Weekly: This is a more tangible goal with defined business impact. Set metrics for improvement, then work with your reps on a plan to applying the necessary skills on a daily basis to achieve this goal. This should be a slightly more involved reward such as a round of golf that will influence meaningful results.
- Monthly: The largest of the three goals, monthly goals are accompanied by higher-value rewards based on extraordinary performance. I prefer not to give cash, because once you spend it, it's gone. Instead, I've given physical SPIFs like speakers and TV sets. Every time your rep looks at that item, they'll remember the process they went through to earn it.

Figure out where the issue lies: There are two main aspects of motivation every sales manager must handle: Individual motivation, and group-wide motivation. Before you do anything to boost motivation, ask yourself, how many people seem like their spirits are flagging? If the answer is just one or two, you're dealing with outliers. If that number is three or more, there's a problem with the entire team.

Communicate: As we previously established, trust is paramount to establishing a relationship with your team and getting their participation, buy-in, and motivation. In order to establish that trust, take a look at how you communicate with your team, both on an individual level and team-wide. You can easily conduct a stand-up meeting in the morning to get your reps' blood pumping, using your energy and enthusiasm to bring up the temperature in the room and start the day off right. You can also conduct one-on-one meetings to really get to know each team member on an individual level and help coach them toward their goals. It also helps to have mini check-ins during the day, whether that's with a short motivational email or an encouraging word when they're not busy.

Overachievement commissions: These are higher rates that kick in after quotas are met. For example, salespeople may earn a penny on a dollar with their regular commission rate until quotas are reached, but earn two pennies on a dollar on all sales above quotas. An overachievement commission rate can help keep stars in the field during the fourth quarter—often the period in which customers are most ready to buy.

Autonomy: When businesses give their employees more flexibility to set their own priorities, schedules, goals, and work habits, teams feel a greater sense of ownership and therefore motivation. Examples of autonomy in the workplace include the ability to telecommute, the freedom for sales reps to set their own hours as long as the work gets done, or offering unlimited vacation days as long as quotas are met. While autonomy over schedule may be more difficult in a call center or customer service setting where hours need to be covered, there are other areas where autonomy can be integrated. Allowing sales or customer service reps to set their own goals and choose their own metrics are examples of intrinsic sales motivation techniques.

Mastery: The second tenet of sales motivation Pink advocates. People don't want to be robots. They want to feel achievement. They want to succeed. Oftentimes, however, they don't know how. It's not that companies don't spend lavish amounts on training their salespeople in sales training seminars, explains Jason Jordan in his book Cracking the Sales Management Code. The problem of mastery comes when sales managers are not equipped with the skills to help their sales teams set and meet the right goals. "With extremely rare exception "the best sales managers we've encountered are unconsciously competent scientists. They hold formal meetings with formal agendas on formal schedules. They set rigorous expectations for their salespeople and track progress against those goals with equal rigor. They manage by analysis rather than anecdote and by measurement rather than gut. They are continuous-improvement experts with action plans galore. A great sales manager, who actually teaches sales teams rather than simply inspects them, can motivate their team to master the skills needed to achieve.

Purpose: The last key to motivating people is purpose. Largely, says Pink, people will achieve more when they serve a purpose larger than themselves. As a company, seek to define a purpose bigger than achieving profit. For example, aim to deliver the best product or service for your customer. Embrace values such as excellence, service, and teamwork. A sense of purpose becomes even clearer when companies team up with charities. Creating a business environment of cooperation is another way to achieve purpose. Gamification, can add to a culture striving for a larger purpose. Some companies have used their CRM dashboards to track personal goals for department-wide or company-wide contests, solidifying relationships in the company. When Gamification is used to help charity, sales incentive programs take on a purpose higher than increasing the bottom line is an excellent motivator.

How to Motivate Sales Team

1. **Measure and Reward behaviors, not results** – Give employees kudos and bonuses not only on the amount of deals they close but also on following up enough times on leads, recoding information on your CRM and doing good detective work prospecting potential clients. This will make sure your team has a clear path to success and make everyone have a shot at getting rewarded.

2. **Celebrate success** – Don't wait for a massive sale to show your team appreciation. On the contrary, celebrating small wins can drive motivation during slump times and keep employees engaged and eager on their day to day tasks. Make sure to pat your team members on the back for small successes like getting in touch with an unresponsive lead on the 5th attempt or finding a new champion with a stagnant opportunity that seemed to be going nowhere.

3. **Celebrate Success II** – Celebrate your client's success as well as your own. Ask clients for feedback, how they use your product and what results are they seeing. Share these stories with your team, send them in internal newsletters and post customer testimonials on your walls. Letting employees know the value of their product or service can be a strong source of motivation.

4. **Virtual Brainstorming** – It takes a village to make a sale. Getting your team together to think about how to approach a certain client or how to structure your sales process will both tap into their team spirit and promote knowledge sharing. Research shows that virtual brainstorming

(e.g. via social feeds or chats) is much more effective than physical as there is less likelihood of pushback, embarrassment or bias.

5. **Set clear goals** – Being lost can feel stressful. Creating clear goals that are challenging yet obtainable will help your team know what they're working for and what constitutes success. Once goals are in place all activities should naturally align. Goals should not be vague, e.g. make lots of sales. They should be short term and directive – e.g. bring 10 new clients from account X by the end of the quarter.

6. **Competitions** – Many salespeople are naturally competitive so tapping into that can be great for motivation. Word of warning though – competition can be alienating if you feel there is no chance to win. Make sure to level the playing field, pitting employees against their equals or against relevant benchmarks. Also, competitions should be short and targeted to stay relevant.

7. **Positive exhibitionism** – When your team members do something well, make sure everybody knows about it. In a company I once worked with, we had a large gong which anyone who made a sale was required to ring (regardless of the deal size). These activities, drive team spirit, boost positive competitiveness and make everyone feel a part of the company success.

8. **Give and request feedback** – An open culture of feedback helps team members know they are appreciated and have some place to turn for coaching and support. Don't wait till your annual review session to tell team members what you think or ask them how they want to be managed. Maintain an open channel of feedback so that your feedback remains relevant and actionable.

9. **Play games** – Gamification, using game mechanics for work, is a great for motivating sales teams. Gamification systems help you set up competitions, provide context for feedback and help you celebrate success. These tools let you control your team's activities without having them feel micromanaged. Adding game mechanics such as points, badges and leaderboards you can allow employees to take an active part in monitoring their own performance and inconspicuously nudge them towards desirable activities

CHAPTER NINE

Overcoming Sales Objections

Arguably the toughest aspect of any sales position is overcoming sales objections. Whether you offer a service or are a small retail business, today's buyers are more discerning than ever. Your goal is to have a convincing response to the roadblocks standing between you and that coveted sale. As many experienced sales people know, most sales calls are met with at least one objection. We've gathered the most common sales objections on budget, authority, need, timeliness, and value — along with steps for how best to overcome each.

It is great to move closer to closing a deal, but there can be bumps in the form of objections in the final stage. But before thinking **about how to overcome the sales objection** of clients? You should know the importance of objection handling. First of all, it is essential to stop seeing a sales objection in a negative light. It can be beneficial to have objections. Objection handling may be the most underrated step in the sales process, but it is crucial. The success of the deal depends on how well you handle the objection. If you do it well, you close the deal and, if you don't, you lose it. Therefore, being a pro in the art of objection handling can make salespeople close more deals successfully.

Listen: Don't just let your prospect spell out their objections – actually *listen*. Chances are you'll be able to anticipate potential objections before they even occur. I'll talk you through the most common concerns – and how to overcome them – later in this article. Rather than jumping in with an answer – or even worse, cutting your prospect off before they've even had time to share their concerns in full – be sure to give your prospect time to speak. It'll help them feel like you're genuinely looking to help and have their best interests at heart, which increases your chances of closing the deal once you've handed the sales objection.

Understand: People are complex. We don't always say exactly what we mean – and even when we try to, our words might still be misinterpreted. So it's important to paraphrase your prospect's concerns to demonstrate that you understand their objection (or that you *didn't* fully understand, therefore giving your prospect the opportunity to correct you). For example, you might say: "Just to be clear that we're on the same page here, you're concerned that the onboarding costs are too high, so it'll take too long – and cost too much – for you to see the benefit of our product. Is that correct? There may also be additional underlying objections that the prospect hasn't voiced, or may only have alluded too. You'll need to ask open-ended questions to help you dig up all the objections before you're in a position to respond effectively.

Respond: Whether or not they seem like a serious issue to you, acknowledge that your prospect's concerns are valid. If they feel like you're not taking the objections seriously or are just trying to steamroller them into an agreement, it's unlikely you'll end up closing the deal. If the objection is something you have the authority to handle yourself, don't be afraid to do it. Otherwise, explain that you need to run it up the flagpole and arrange a time to get back to them.

Confirm: Reiterate the objection and confirm that if you're able to overcome it, the prospect will be happy to move forward with the deal. This second part is really important: there's no point in taking the time to overcome a sales objection if it *still* won't move you any closer to securing their business. Remember that some prospects are simply never going to buy – in which case it's not an objection, it's a brush-off. If they don't have sufficient budget, aren't a fully qualified prospect, or lack the authority to make a decision – and show no signs of discussing your pitch with anyone higher up the chain of command – then you're likely wasting your time.

Overcoming Specific Objections

Now's Not a Good Time: Timing is a common problem, for several reasons. In fact, there are actually two objections hiding in here: 1) I personally don't have time to handle this, and 2) This is really not a good time to buy.

Either way, you need to investigate further to know how to proceed.

How to Handle It

If the prospect thinks that now is not a good time to buy, consider these aspects before continuing:

1. Make sure prospect is qualified (don't waste *your* time)
2. Don't oversell because you're feeling desperate

It's Too Expensive: A sales objection to price is not as straightforward as it sounds. Sure, there could truly be a lack of cash. But it could also be a brush-off, or the prospect might not think that your product is a good enough value to justify the cost.

How to Handle It

Again, you'll need to work to uncover the real reasons behind the objection. Try pausing for several seconds after a prospect has objected to price, as they'll often volunteer more information unprompted. Once they've finished talking, ask a few more questions to really zero in on their objection. Try to find out what makes the prospect think your product or service is expensive (or too expensive in comparison to an alternative). You'll often find their issue is more of a vague feeling than anything concrete. In this case, a few hard facts may help put their mind at ease. If you feel that the prospect just needs a little reassurance, put the price in context (how much it costs in relation to ROI, how much it would cost *not* to act, etc). It's less about proving the product is worth the price than it is about demonstrating its value. Once your product seems crucial, the price will matter less.

I'm Already in Another Contract: Here's an easy one for you. The contractual objection is a straightforward concern, with a relatively simple answer.

How to Handle It

You have a lot of room for flexibility here, but it depends on what your prospect is thinking. Genuinely interested prospects might be afraid of cash flow problems if they're already in another contract, while others simply don't like feeling trapped. If a prospect has a genuine need for your product, a discount or creative payment schedule might overcome their sales objection. This will depend greatly on how happy they are with their current contract, so ask them straight out if they're satisfied or want a change. And if all else fails? Mark your calendar to follow up (assuming they're a good prospect) a few weeks before their existing contract expires when they're likely to be evaluating their renewal.

Just Send Me the Info: Comments like "Just send me your information" or "Call me at X point in the future," can be interpreted in two ways, depending on whether they're said early or late in the call.

How to Handle It

If you hear this kind of dismissal early in the call, it's probably a brush-off. Double-check your lead qualification workflow to see how an unsuitable candidate made it onto your list. If it's said later in the call, the problem may stem from the lead being too busy or not really understanding the benefits of your product. If you think the latter is true, take another look at your presentation. If your leads don't understand what you're selling, there's a fatal flaw in your marketing.

I Don't Have Time to Talk to You Right Now: Even though this objection sounds like a brush-off, it's probably true – no one has time for anything extra these days. If your target is simply too busy, there's no guaranteed solution, but at least your options are pretty straightforward.

How to Handle It

First, try to discover if it's really a lack of time, or if it's something else. Using the general sales objection process above, the interaction might go like this:

I'm sorry, I just don't have time to talk to you today.

- **Listen** – Employ active listening.
- **Understand** – I completely understand. I'm swamped too, and this is a crazy time of year.
- **Respond** – I really don't want to waste your time. I can tell you about the product in three minutes flat. If you're interested, I'll send you more information, and if you're not, we'll leave it at that.
- **Confirm** – Great, so no more than three minutes of your time. How does that sound?

    - **If your prospect says yes** – "Terrific, can I go ahead now?"
    - **If they say no** – "I'm looking at my calendar – how about this afternoon at 3 o'clock?"

If the answer is still no, you're going to have to probe deeper to find out what's going on. If you're still struggling to find a way around the objection, consider that the target might indeed have a need, but the urgency of meeting that need isn't great or has waned since they first entered your funnel. If that's the case, you'll need to reevaluate that person's journey to this point, as you may have missed something that's now making them view the problem as less important.

I Need to Run This Past My Boss: Whether or not you'll encounter this objection tends to depend on company size. In larger companies, people will tell you "I need to run it past my boss" or "I need to discuss it with colleagues." In smaller companies, you can add "I need to run it by my partner" to the list.

How to Handle It

Again, this one is fairly straightforward. If a prospect really isn't authorized to make the decision, ask to speak to the person who is and start again. If they are, but will still have to "sell" your product internally, you can actually help them prepare for likely objections with answers and solutions to smooth the process.

Product X is Cheaper: Every so often, a target will attempt to shut you down by referring to your competitors. This is a blessing in disguise, because a true comparison with a competitor gives you the chance to spot overlooked opportunities and spark new ideas. There's also a good chance the target already knows what they need (since they've been talking to/ researching the competition), which saves you time too.

How to Handle It

Ask questions to explore their relationship with the competitor or the offer they've been made. They might not be persuaded to switch to your product or service, but look at it as a learning experience – and if they mention problems that your product *can* solve, you might make the sale regardless.

You Don't Offer Feature X: These days, people are used to – and expect – personalization from all products. Sometimes that's possible, and sometimes it isn't. If it's not, you can still go a long way toward making the prospect *feel* like your product or service is personalized by giving them extra time in your interactions and actively listening.

How to Handle It

Sure, customize where possible, to the extent you're able to. But also realize that if your prospect needs something you can't provide, they might not be a good fit after all.

I Need to get a Few More Quotes: The shopping around sales objection is frustrating, but very common. Remember that it can hide multiple objections – it may either be a gentle brush-off, or the truth may be that the target *is* actually shopping around.

How to Handle It

This type of sales objection seems to be best overcome using a solid script to work around the situation. If someone really believes that they need other quotes (a common approach to buying), it's unlikely you'll be able to deter them. As always, if you're using sales scripts and other resources to help you handle certain problems, practice enough that you can be flexible and natural when dealing with prospects.

You Have a Bad Review: Dealing with negative word of mouth or bad reviews is a great opportunity for growth. You can't make bad publicity disappear, but you can learn from it and improve in the future.

How to Handle It

Surprisingly, this is a fairly easy fix, as long as you're proactive. Don't try to avoid the issue – directly address the problem or concern as quickly as possible. If it's an issue that someone in-house is already working on fixing, offer to put the prospect in touch with them to allay their fears and answer any questions. Likewise, if you can offer some kind of reassurance and explanation, do so. Once you've explained the issue and what the company is doing to fix or avoid these problems in the future, follow up with a perk or value-add to take the sting out of the experience.

Where the Hell Did You Get My Name?: Most salespeople will face an aggressive prospect at some point or another. Some people are just unpleasant, and there's not much you can do about it. But remember – unhappy customers tell more people about their experience than happy ones do, so resist the temptation to sink to their level.

How to Handle It

Kill with calmness and kindness. Some complaints, like "Where did you get my number?" can be answered directly. Other situations may result from personality clashes. If this is the case, can you hand off the prospect to a colleague or use a psychology-based technique?

Finally, realize that some people just cannot be won over. Stay calm and collected and try to diffuse the tension, but never let yourself get drawn into the melee.

No One's Home: This isn't technically an objection, but it can have the same effect on your prospecting efforts: What happens when you can't get your prospect to respond to you?

How to Handle It

The key here is balance and knowing when to call it quits. First, use the right channel – there's no point in calling if your prospect is an email-only type. Second, be persistent. People are busy and salespeople are usually not a priority. That said, know when it's time to call it quits – preferably *before* you become an annoyance.

Be proactive when overcoming sales objections: As a sales professional, it's absolutely necessary to understand and be prepared for the most common sales objections. Knowing every detail and feature of your product or service is important, but getting into the true core of the customer's objection is equally crucial. Respectfully ask your buyer open-ended questions that probe deeper into what's behind their objection. With an understanding of your customer's wants and needs and your product's offerings, you can work on overcoming sales objections based on budget, authority, need, time, and value. Above all, remember that your goal is to convince the potential buyer that they can't, or shouldn't, live without your product or service. The art of sales is inherently associated with objections, but most can be overcome by building a sense of credibility, trust, and re framing the way your buyer sees what you're selling. When it comes down to it, sales is about showing the product/service at the angle that's best-suited to the conversation.

CHAPTER TEN

Presentation Skills

An important part of leadership is having a strong vision and purpose, and demonstrating these through actions and leadership style. Equally important in leadership is the ability to communicate this purpose and vision to the organisation and staff in a confident and persuasive manner. Leaders can be knowledgeable and competent in their work and have a strong vision, but they struggle if they cannot clearly and effectively articulate and present their ideas and vision to those who need to hear it. The ability to speak and present like a leader, and earn the trust and commitment of staff and colleagues are essential to those in a leadership position. It's essential to be able to influence the audience and bring them to the speaker's point of view.

You could be communicating one-on-one to direct reports or on mass to your employees, shareholders or other external stakeholders. In either case, as a leader you must make sure your presentation skills are accomplished enough to ensure the message you are delivering resonates appropriately in all these instances. Having the ability to speak doesn't necessarily make us good at it. Anyone can share information. Whether our content is clearly understood is an entirely different matter. Some leaders think that there are no technical competencies attached to communication. That belief fuels the myth that communication doesn't affect the financial success of their business. There is often an assumption that just because we can speak well during an interview, we can all communicate effectively.

Problem: Poor communication is a bit like high blood pressure. If you neglect it for too long the consequences can be disastrous. At school we are taught to read, remember and repeat. We learn a wide range of skills, although, effective communication is often one of them.

Some of us move on to higher education and the growing pressure to pass exams increases exponentially. We learn to read, remember and repeat at a much higher level. How much time is invested in helping us to speak with confidence, clarity and impact? We leave school, graduate from college or university and suddenly find ourselves in a new world. It's a world where the most important skill we need to survive let alone thrive is communication. One day we are asked to present our work or ideas to colleagues or customers and the panic sets in. It's no wonder that so many people have some anxiety about public speaking.

Be confident: Believe in yourself and what you are trying to achieve. Your self-belief will shine through to those you are trying to engage and influence. This is particularly so if the audience is a challenging one. If they sense any self-doubt, you'll fail on both counts. The words that follow are those of a storyteller rather than a leading management guru but they sum this point up well. We are touching on mindset as much as communication here but know the reason for your vision and the ideas that sit behind it. Why are they important to you? Why do you believe in them, and more significantly, why you want others to believe in them too? Keep these in mind, especially for those occasions when your vision is challenged. If you keep your self-belief intact you are much more likely to take your audience with you, even if they are reluctant converts.

Create trust: Trust begins with honesty, openness and transparency. Invest as much time and energy as you can encouraging your team to speak openly. Create a culture where everyone's voice is valued and respected. Nurture an environment where people can feel and be themselves. Assure your team that they don't have to edit everything they say just because you are the boss.

Start connecting: Every organisation has its own internal communication culture. Much of the 'corporate speak' our teams hear every day isn't very helpful. Stop churning out emails and updates in a language that very few people understand. It's not how most people speak themselves. Only send it to those who it's completely relevant to. Make it personal, human, relevant and engaging. Whether you are writing it or saying it, make sure that it's focused on connecting with the team.

Show vulnerability: If you want your team to present their ideas with passion, purpose and energy, lead the way. Show them how to do it first. Help them how to be open and know that it's fine to feel vulnerable. Show them how to lighten up, relax and not take everything so seriously. Help them to be themselves rather than simply their job title. Avoid the 'corporate speak' by being yourself. And show them that's how you want them to be too.

Keep it conversational: No one likes to be lectured to. As leaders we each have an opportunity to connect with our teams in a far more conversational manner. Keep your message personal, focused and tailored to the people you are speaking with. Involve them, and ask them how they feel.

Feelings matter: Be absolutely clear before you begin to speak how you want people to feel. How do you want them to feel?

– The moment you begin to speak

– All the time they are with you

– The moment they walk out of the door

Most people will forget most of what you said by the time they return to their desk. They won't however, forget how you made them feel. Please keep in mind that there is nothing 'soft' or easy about communicating effectively. It's one of the hardest things we have to do every day. Help your team to get good at it. Give them the presentation skills to speak with confidence.

Preparation eliminates fear: Delivering information, particularly if it's in front of an audience, can be a daunting task. In fact public speaking is often listed as one of the most common fears that people have, so common in fact that there's a name for it. Glossophobia in psychology is the name for the fear of public speaking. If you are like the majority of people who have apprehensions about presenting then remember that fear is good news, it's the minds way of highlighting areas in your life that lack information. It's natural when you are unaware of an outcome that the mind automatically imagines a negative outcome. It's a mechanism to protect us from harm. The best way to eliminate any sense of fear or apprehension is to provide clarity about the outcome so the more you prepare your presentation and the more you deliver presentations the more the feeling of fear naturally goes away.

Identify the action you want: The purpose of a presentation should never be to convey information but instead to encourage a particular course of action. As a leader you need to identity what you want the listener to do as a result of your presentation e.g. work harder, increase sales, increase budget etc. This needs to be at the center of your preparation. A presentation that just informs people is a waste of time. An effective presentation is one that inspires action.

Prepare a ten second summary: No matter how long your presentation is whether it's five minutes or fifty minutes you need to have a ten second version of your presentation, a simple line that summarises the whole presentation. This should be mentioned at least three times within your presentation. The famed scientist Albert Einstein once said "If you can't explain it simply, you don't understand it well enough" the best leaders are able to take complex ideas and make them simple enough for everyone to understand, not only does this make the action you want more likely to occur but you will find that your message will spread far easier, making your scope of influence far wider.

Use imaginary: The mind is much more likely to remember images than words. Everyone would have had a time when they went to a meeting and met someone only to forget their name and you would have thought to yourself "I know the face but I can't quite remember the name" yet I highly doubt that anyone experienced telling anyone "I know your name but I can't remember your face." It's because we remember imagery than we do words so every effective presentation has a Leader that is able to tell a story that creates images in the minds of the audience that illustrates the purpose of the presentation.

Change your tone: If you want to influence people it's always more effective to do this in person than via an email or a report. That's because the written words don't convey tone, the use of tone can dramatically alter how the message is received and it can turn a positive into a negative and visa versa. A couple of things to focus on during your presentation is firstly slow down when staying your key message and leave a small gap between each word. This is called "blocking." In the mind of the audience it places more importance on that statement. Secondly when you want to raise emotion you have to raise the level of your tone.

CHAPTER ELEVEN

Proposal Writing

Knowing how to write an effective sales proposal is an essential skill for sales professionals. A sales proposal communicates the value of your business's products and services to potential buyers. Learning about the steps you can take to write a sales proposal can help make your next business pitch more successful. In this article, we discuss sales proposals and provide steps, a template and an example to help you write this document. A sales proposal is a written business document that pitches a product or service to prospective customers and clients. An effective business proposal identifies a need or problem experienced by the target audience and explains how the product or service fulfills those needs. The document also incorporates specific details, such as costs and deliverables, to help ensure the audience has sufficient information to decide on the purchase.

Writing sales proposals of quality, value and credibility is an involved process but is an invaluable skill for sales managers and sales people looking for improved results. Writing Sales Proposals, another comprehensive and informative business skills training course from Maguire Training, takes delegates step-by-step through the process of creating highly-effective sales proposals which contain everything the potential customer is looking for in order to make a favorable purchasing decision. There is no quick and easy route to perfecting the effective sales proposal other than formal training, but for anyone whose daily role involves writing proposals this handy guide from Maguire Training gives you the essential information required to improve the most important aspects for more effective sales proposals.

Readability is of the utmost importance: Firstly, a sales proposal should be easy to read and understand. Information should be presented in bite-sized chunks with no more than one or two subjects per paragraph. A clear, readable font such as Arial or Verdana should be used. Paragraphs should be led by a clear an emboldened header which states the subject(s) covered. Spacing and graphics should be used appropriately to break up text, and page layouts should not be demanding on the eye.

Content must be customer-focused: It can be tempting to turn a sales proposal into a PR exercise for your business, but the best sales proposals are all about the customer and demonstrate that their needs have been listened to, understood and addressed in detail.

There are a number of ways in which the content of an effective sales proposal can be written to demonstrate customer focus. Always refer to the customer by name in your proposal, giving it greater prominence than references to your own business. State clearly the desired outcome expressed by the customer as a result of purchasing from you. List each of the customer's specific problems, challenges and issues in order of importance to the customer and precisely but succinctly explain how your product or service is the ideal solution for each. Emphasize the benefits of your offering to the customer, rather than detailing its features.

Sales proposals should be tailored appropriately: Whilst there's no harm in creating a generic sales proposal template, it is vital that this is tailored in accordance with each individual customer's need. For example, your 'base' proposal may include technical data and specifications which may be meaningless if your customer has insufficient technical knowledge. Similarly, the language used should be tailored to ensure ease of understanding by the recipient. Ambiguous phrasing and overuse of technical jargon should be avoided. The information required by the customer and upon which they will base their purchasing decision should be obvious and easily found in the document and any claims made for your solution relevant to your customer's requirements should be backed up by real-world evidence.

Edit and review your proposal: Just because you're done writing your proposal doesn't mean it's ready for your buyer's eyes. Don't send a proposal to your prospects without proofreading yourself and securing necessary approvals. Proofread your proposal and cross-reference it with your research on the buyer and the sales cycle so far. Ensure all information about the solution and pricing aligns with any previous discussions you've had with the buyer to avoid any surprises when they receive your proposal.

Seek out necessary internal stakeholders to review your proposal before sending it out. Your sales operations team can check that your pricing is accurate. Your customer success team can confirm your timeline for onboarding the buyer. Enlisting the help of other teams can help catch any errors in your proposal you may have missed. An accurate proposal helps present the best version of your business to a buyer. Allow time for feedback on your proposal to create a better buyer experience.

Use sales proposals to win more customers: Sales proposals are a vital piece of sales collateral that outline your proposed solution to a potential customer. The best sales proposals help your sales team win a deal, but they take time, effort and collaboration to get right.

Proposals combine forces of sales, marketing, customer success and product teams to present the most accurate information to a potential buyer. Proposals arrive after a pitch or demo to summarize past conversations and provide a clear roadmap for a solution to the buyer's challenge. Creating a winning sales proposal starts with gathering information about the prospect and similar use cases. Then, sales teams can use past proposals or proposal templates to outline and draft the content itself. Finally, the proposal gets approval from internal stakeholders before finally being sent to the buying team.

A sales proposal has three basic objectives.

First, it educates the prospective client about the full nature of his need. Often, a prospective client may be aware of only a portion of his need. This may be a perfect opportunity for you to demonstrate your ability to see "the forest from the trees" as an objective third-party expert.

Second, the proposal convinces the prospect that you have the competence to deliver what he needs, better than he can himself.

Third, the proposal provides justification for the prospect's investment in terms that are useful and understandable to the client.

However, to convince your client that you are the best person for the job, you must get him to read your proposal. So how do you get this busy executive to lay aside other pressing issues and pick up your proposal? The answer is to write a proposal that satisfies his needs, not one that sells your services. And to do that, you must have a full understanding of the nature, scope and needs of the prospect and present your ideas in a manner that convinces the prospect that your product or service represents the best way to handle his needs.

Keep in mind...You must convey the feeling that you are the expert to all who read the proposal.

The proposal must showcase your value to your prospect's organization. You have to convince your prospect why he cannot fulfill his needs with resources internal to his organization.

You must differentiate your goods or services from the competition — if you can first show your prospect that he needs external resources to satisfy his needs, then you must convince him that you are the best choice for the job.

The proposal offers value-added solutions. Organizations are not interested in novelty approaches. They have problems that need solutions...quick! The winning proposal will outline how a client can solve his problems and achieve his objectives, as well as look good to the rest of the organization — especially his boss.

CHAPTER TWELVE

Prospecting and lead generation

Sales prospecting and lead generation are two essential aspects of running a successful enterprise of any size. They're intuitive business development strategies that help nurture the target audience and transform them into paying customers. These two techniques often work in conjunction with one another, but many fail to understand that they are distinct processes that need different courses of action. Sales prospecting and lead generation techniques have subtle differences. Knowing the distinction between the two can help businesses understand which one to focus on to address specific needs.

Sales Prospecting vs Lead Generation: The main difference between prospecting and lead generation is that the former is a sales function, while the latter is a marketing strategy. Sales prospecting is a short-term, 1:1 method that concentrates on a defined set of prospective customers within the business's target market. It's usually the first step in the sales funnel, and it entails identifying and engaging with leads to create sales opportunities.

Prospecting makes use of manual and personalized marketing tactics, such as email campaigns and cold calls. The sales representatives typically must contact leads who have lost contact with the brand. They also have to develop a database of prospects and communicate with them to convert them into sales. Lead generation is a long-term strategy that focuses on building brand awareness and staying on top of mind. It's a one-to-many approach that keeps the audience interested in what the business has to offer. It helps develop a sales pipeline and keep it healthy. Lead generation mainly uses automated processes and focuses on people who have expressed interest in the brand's products and services, rather than just people who qualify as potential customers. As its name suggests, it just highlights getting leads, whereas prospecting involves finding clients and nurturing leads into closed sales.

Sales prospecting is the process of identifying and contacting potential new customers, known as prospects. A prospect is any individual or organization that's a good fit for and can benefit from your solution. Prospecting activities are the first stage of the sales process and are carried out by sales teams. Mostly, but not exclusively, sales development representatives (SDRs). Account executives (AEs) also prospect in many companies. Sales prospectors seek out, contact, and qualify prospects with the aim of setting up meetings with their AEs, who then take over and guide prospects through the sales funnel until they close the deal.

Sales prospecting is a very time-consuming process involving a lot of different activities. Some happen at the level of the company or sales team, others are down to individual salespeople.

Here are just a few:

Tasks carried out at company or sales team level, or by a product marketer if your company has one:

- Calculating your total addressable market (TAM, the total number of prospects available in your target market).
- Creating an ideal customer profile (ICP) with firmographics and technographics of the target customer company.
- Creating buyer personas (BP) profiling individual roles, responsibilities, and challenges, and how your solution can solve them.

- Researching prospects and their challenges using sales prospecting tools like ZoomInfo, Diffbot, etc., databases, and online sources.

Tasks carried out by individual sales reps:

- Tracking industry news, company hirings, prospect job changes, etc. using B2B sales prospecting tools like LinkedIn Sales Navigator to identify sales opportunities and determine the best time for outreach.

- Social selling. So, identifying and engaging with prospects on social media, sending LinkedIn messages, etc. to warm prospects up before outreach.

- Qualifying inbound leads from marketing before placing them in the sales pipeline. This involves reaching out to determine whether they genuinely need your product and have the authority to buy, so you don't waste time and resources on lukewarm leads.

- Performing cold outreach via email, phone, etc.

- Scripting sales and setting an agenda for meetings.

- Booking client meetings with AEs.

- Taking the time to listen to prospects, understand their challenges, and build relationships.

- Using a sales engagement platform like Mixmax to run multi-channel prospecting sequences, customize sales prospecting email templates with prospect data from your CRM, and leverage features like best-time-of-day scheduling, easy calendar scheduling, etc. to maximize the chances of getting a response.
- Asking existing customers for referrals.

Lead generation?

Lead generation is carried out by the marketing team to build brand awareness, generate interest in and demand for a product, and capture contact information to build prospecting and marketing lists.

Lead generation strategies aim to create a consistent pipeline of leads that have a high chance of converting into customers following qualification and nurturing by the sales team. Inbound leads are known as marketing qualified leads (MQL) since they've demonstrated interest in your product and company by interacting with you in some way.

Some tactics in the marketer's arsenal include:

Preparation:

- Researching customer pain points.
- Creating marketing buyer personas, which usually include more demographic and personal data than sales BPs.

- Identifying which channels potential customers use, and how to best engage them.
- Identifying what content they consume and how.
- Creating landing pages and online forms to capture inbound contact information when someone signs up for a webinar or newsletter, or downloads a lead magnet.

Outbound activities:

- Performing content marketing activities, like creating lead magnets—white papers, video tutorials, blogs, etc.—and sharing them via email, social media, on the company website, etc.
- Performing account-based marketing using tools like Triblio, which enable marketers to reach out to prospects in the same target account with content personalized for them.
- Using marketing automation tools to carry out streamlined, repeatable one-to-many outreach. For example, email marketing via Mailchimp to share event invites, product announcements, offers, company milestones, and more.
- Lead nurturing: Sharing content designed to generate desire for your product with leads who aren't yet ready to buy.

Differences between sales prospecting and lead generation
Sales prospecting and lead generation are both designed to pack your pipeline with prospects, but they differ in several ways.

- Sales prospecting is a short-term process designed to generate results faster than lead generation, which tends to be a slower, more long-term strategy.

- Prospecting is a highly focused, hyper-personalized activity targeting a relatively small group of people. Think of us as sales process snipers. And while lead generation isn't exactly spraying bullets, it targets a much wider audience to generate a larger volume of contacts.

- Inbound leads are aware of your company on some level and have demonstrated intent and interest by interacting with your content, which makes starting a conversation and converting them easier.

Prospects, on other hand, don't yet know you, even though they may need your product, which means conversions take longer. And there's no guarantee of success. You might target the right person with the right solution, but for one reason or another, they're just not in a position to buy.

***However*, outbound prospecting does give you more control over who you interact with.** With lead generation, you can put out messaging targeting a specific industry or persona, but you have limited control over who responds. If you're swamped with requests for demos and meetings from leads that don't fit your ICP or don't have authority to buy, they could eat into your time and resources without resulting in a sale.

And while MQLs from inbound marketing campaigns are warm leads, they still need to be qualified by sales to check whether they're worth pursuing. By contrast, outbound prospecting allows you to pick prospects you know could benefit from your solution. So these leads are often more valuable, and the resulting deals tend to be larger.

- Lead generation is one-way communication that's all about your product. Good prospecting, on the other hand, should be all about the customer, with a lot of two-way communication and sales prospecting techniques like a high listen-to-talk ratio to establish trust.
- With lead generation, there's little immediate engagement beyond the automated response that lands in your inbox seconds after you download a lead magnet.

Prospecting, however, involves a lot more personalization and one-to-one engagement via email, phone and video calls, LinkedIn messaging, etc. When a prospect engages with content shared via Mixmax, real-time engagement alerts mean they'll get a personalized follow-up call from the sales rep.

The amount of engagement and personalization means there's a lot to keep on top of. That's why busy sales teams use tools like Mixmax to personalize multi-channel outreach at scale.

It's a never-ending simulation that is costing your business time and money. Marketing and sales alignment is essential to the success of your business. Here are the best ways to begin the alignment process:

- **Determine lead requirements**: Establish what comprises a marketing qualified lead (MQL) and sales qualified lead (SQL) to eliminate confusion.
- **Develop a service level agreement** (SLA): An SLA is a contract between your sales and marketing team meant to hold both departments accountable. It should clearly outline marketing and sales responsibilities.
- **Implement a lead scoring system**: This assigns a predetermined value to specific actions taken by leads. Once a lead has reached the point threshold, it's ready to hand off to sales.
- **Specify the handoff point**: Once a lead becomes an MQL, marketing hands it off to the sales team. However, what categorizes a lead as *qualified* is unique to each business.

Lead Generation vs. Sales Prospecting: The Difference

Misaligned marketing and sales teams can waste time and cause leads to go unused. For a successful sales process, both departments *must work together*.

Marketing can help sales teams speed up the sales cycle through lead generation strategies that focus on higher-quality contacts.

There will be less confusion if you have clearly defined lead qualification criteria, and the marketing-to-sales handoff will go smoother.

Just remember lead generation ≠ sales prospecting.

Lead generation and sales prospecting work together to achieve a same company goal to increase sales. And the reality is, whether you recognize the distinction between these two processes or use the terms interchangeably, getting your sales and marketing departments to work together toward a common goal is the most important component of expanding your organization. Sales prospecting and lead generation work well in synchrony, but it's best to keep their differences in mind to utilize these powerful strategies properly. Knowing which one to focus on will help your business address its needs and achieve its short-term and long-term goals. With the proper tools and techniques, you'll be able to drive your brand forward.

Which Method is the Most Appropriate for your Business?: First and foremost, establish your Ideal Customer Profile. Choosing your objectives, overall sales strategy, and which tools to employ becomes a lot easier once you know who you're targeting. Prospecting and lead creation should be done at the same time, as we mentioned previously. However, this isn't always the best option. For example, your sales staff may find themselves with a depleted lead pipeline that urgently need replenishment. Prospecting makes the most sense in this scenario. If your pipeline is strong, however, investing time, energy, and money in lead generation is the best long-term option, as it will yield better, more qualified prospects to work with down the road. That is all there is to it.

CHAPTER THIRTEEN

Sales Fundamentals

What do the successful sales initiatives of multi-billion dollar enterprises, early-stage start-ups, tech and healthcare companies all have in common? Every time, the success of the sales effort often comes down to consistent execution of the fundamentals. This shouldn't be surprising. In baseball, especially the playoffs, experts often note how key games come down to things as simple as catching and throwing the ball. Or running the bases. Fundamentals that are easy to overlook, yet can make or break your success. It's no different in sales. There are no shortcuts, and the fundamentals that will drive success can just as easily be forgotten, or ignored, or brushed aside when things get particularly busy. So if we go by these definitions fundamentals is the foundation and origin of a skill or system, not the skill or system itself. Here is the problem- when the discussion was brought up, the majority of the answers from sales leaders and manager talked about skills and competencies, the end result, not the foundation of what creates those skills and competencies. Don't mistake me, all these things are important. But they are not the fundamentals, they are not the unchanging foundation of what makes a great salesperson.

Sales fundamentals are about mastering the mindset that allows a salesperson to learn any skill, methodology, tool and buying process so that they are relevant, transparent, and more helpful to the buyer than their website is. Fundamentals comes down to:

1. **Supportive Beliefs:** We all grow up with a set of personal beliefs. How we were raised to behave and what we were taught to think influences and shapes our belief system. What your internal voice tells you will influence your sales behaviors and will either support or hinder your success. Some beliefs will limit or encourage a strong self-image and relationship with prospects. Others will influence buying decisions, size

of deals, and for managers and executives, how they manage people and processes.

2. Lack of need for approval: Do you believe that people need to like you to buy from you? If so, you are setting yourself up for failure. Your fear of being disliked inhibits all of the necessary sales skills to engage in meaningful conversations that win deals. Without a need for approval, you have the freedom to do or say anything.

3. Ability to control emotions: Being emotionally involved in a sale takes you out of the present. You think about the future, or next step. You are not in the present moment and hearing what your prospect is actually saying, including the tone and inflection of their voice. You are losing your objectivity, ability to offer insight, and developing happy ears that tell you what you want to hear. (They're ready to buy!) This will inhibit your ability to listen and ask questions with ease. You will also likely get frustrated and try to "move things along" only to push away prospects with your tactics.

4. Supportive buy cycle: If you are the type of person who has to compare features, price shop, or delays decisions to think a purchase over, then you can certainly understand it when a prospect wants to do the same thing, right? How you behave as a buyer will impact your ability to sell, and if you are a leader, the way you buy will influence how your team sells.

5. Be comfortable discussing money: When your prospect pushes back that you are too expensive, you are likely to agree with them. Instead of helping a prospect focus on the value of solving the problem, you are focused on price. When that happens, you aren't able to find the real budget for a solution. When you focus on price, you are not asking the right questions to make sure you understand the problem. To you, the problem is the price. You can understand that, it seems like a pretty high price to you too.

6. Handling rejection: The ability to handle rejection stems from your own self-image. When you are comfortable with who you are and the value that you bring, you understand that it's not you they reject, just your offer to help. When rejection no longer inhibits you, you will be able to ask the appropriate thought provoking questions and become a thought leader and trusted adviser in your prospects' and clients' mind.

7. **Customer focus:** It's really easy to shift into talking about yourself, your product, your perspective. But if you force yourself to keep the

customer's perspective, you're far more likely to drive interest, credibility and momentum from all of your efforts – prospecting, qualifying, presentations and closing.

8. **Rational optimism:** Think of this as a general approach to the huge volume of "no" answers sales gets on a daily and weekly basis. You can't be successful in sales if you're pessimistic about your chances of success. But you can also set yourself up for failure if you expect too much success. For example, if you expect 75% of your sales pipeline to close, that might not be realistic. Expecting a deal that's close to sign by the end of the month is a great goal, but make sure the elements are in place to make that happen (agreement on price, procurement is involved, etc.).

9. **Tenacity:** While it's important to know when you get a final "no" from the prospect, it's equally important to keep pushing when others might give up. Identify, isolate and address the specific obstacles in the way of your prospect achieving what they want, and buying. Be persistent when the prospect goes dark (often they're still interested, and your persistence is what they need to keep it top of mind). Be relentless in pursuing the objectives of your clients and prospects, as well as the hard work you need to do every day to exceed quota.

10. **Activities:** Sales organizations that focus purely on activities are often being short-sighted. But organizations that don't look at all at activities are missing the very root of success for any consistently performing sales professional. This doesn't mean you're making 120 dials a day. Maybe your goal is to reach out to five new prospects every day, and follow-up with five prospects every day from the previous week. Hitting that number on a daily basis still takes a level of focus & discipline that few people actually have. But hitting those activities, consistently, could be THE most important thing you do to feed your pipeline and meet your quota.

11. **SALES TEAM HABITS:** Good habits are the bedrock of greatness. Planning your time, refining your message, securing next steps, asking for the business. These habits are deeply ingrained in the world's most successful sales people. We start embedding these right away, giving your new teams the best foot forward.

The challenge is that unless you have a unifying concept that pulls all of these elements together, you wind up chasing random acts of enablement. In other words, sales training programs roll out without clear direction, sales tools get designed that only increase complexity, and initiatives to create new insights languish until their sponsor moves on to something more interesting.

First, there are customer roles: That's right. We are starting with the customer, not the sales rep. This is because the role of the sales person is ALWAYS defined by the customer first. Different customers require different sales roles. You cannot create a one-size-fits-all definition of sales role because you do not have one-size-fits-all customers. The best definition of customer roles is not simply about building a generic persona. It is building a customizable persona. Sure, there are some very common patterns to these roles (like job title, background, expectations by altitude), but there should be a place for role to be adjusted for the situation.

Define your sales roles to match customer roles: In other words, do your sales people know how to "switch hats" for different kinds of customers? Have you defined what those hats are – or are your sales people doing that on their own? Your sales roles should be very specific in both what you expect AND how you expect customer conversations to be different. We worked with one client who actually mapped the approach to every single customer profile and made the sales roles align to each one, defining the differences for each. It was detailed work, but the rewards were amazing. Not only did customers get MUCH better experiences (and of course better sales results), it changed how that client approached the recruiting, selecting/promoting, training, and rewards/recognition of their sales force. They were also able to diagnose where conversations broke down – by altitude, by topic, and even by role. The clarity enabled them to finally tackle the issue of engineering relevant conversations.

Apply the same logic to using resources and information: Sadly, most organizations spend massive amounts of time and money on generic marketing and sales initiatives that create irrelevant conversations. All because they didn't understand how vital clear customer and sales roles are to anchoring their use of behaviors/resources/information. Pause. Can you identify which resources, behaviors, and information are needed to maximize the interaction between customer roles and sales roles? And if you can't make that identification, how do you know where to "help?" Or, sadly, does your "help" come across as random acts of enablement?

Do NOT stop defining roles at the frontline/sales representative level. Carry your efforts all the way through to your sales management roles. Seriously, this is a big deal. If you do not define the role of sales manager, as it relates to BOTH customer and sales rep, you will experience what far too many organizations struggle with – sales managers who are really just super sales reps. They do not enlarge the capacity of the team. They do not develop the talent of the future. They do not focus on the larger strategic picture and broader portfolio of market opportunity. Because their role is not defined to do that.

Creating Opportunities: Sales Fundamentals

Closing: It may seem odd that closing is the first fundamental. It's important to understand that sales is made up of conversations and commitments. Once you realize that acquiring a meeting requires you to gain the commitment of time, you understand why this fundamental skill is crucial. Without the ability to gain commitments, B2B sales is difficult.

Targeting: To maximize your efficiency and effectiveness, it's important to target the companies with the greatest likelihood to need help improving their results. When you start prospecting, one of the best uses of your time is to create a list of companies that need your help and will pay for whatever you sell to improve their outcomes.

Prospecting: This is a vital fundamental and the skill most critical to creating new opportunities. Though this will always be true, anyone who avoids this work is nowhere near as successful as those who prospect some part of their day. Whether you are using a prospecting sequence or banging out cold calls, prospecting is a critical activity and skill.

Resolving Concerns: Imagine a busy person is facing a calendar that is overwhelmed with meetings and other commitments. When you call such a prospective client, you can expect them to avoid adding to their agenda. To gain a first meeting, you must resolve the client's concern by explaining the value they will gain by meeting with you.

Storytelling to Compel Change: The stories salespeople tell aren't often helpful for their clients, as most of them try to prove that their company and what they sell will work for the prospective client. The fundamentals of B2B sales require stories about what's changed and why the client will need to evolve to improve their results. This skill is necessary before executing a first meeting.

Creating Value: The easiest way to create value for your prospective clients is to recognize what decision-makers and their teams need from a conversation with a salesperson. The more you educate your prospective client and help them make a good decision, the more valuable your conversation.

Executing a First Meeting: The first meeting is an audition, a sort of tryout to explore whether you might be a good person to help the client make necessary improvements. The two fundamentals that precede this one, storytelling and creating value, must be enabled before a first meeting.

Scheduling a Second Meeting: Recently, it has become more difficult for salespeople to schedule a second meeting. When they do acquire a second meeting, it is likely to be canceled, or the salesperson gets ghosted. The only way to acquire a second meeting is to create enough value in the first meeting to prove you are someone worth the client's time.

Capturing Opportunities

Once you have created an opportunity, you must master another list of fundamental skills that will allow you to win the client's business and capture the opportunity.

Building Consensus: In many B2B sales, you will encounter a large number of stakeholders who will weigh in on the buying decision, including what salesperson is best for helping the organization change. Leaving these people out of the discovery process is often a mistake because they may oppose the plan for improvements.

Discovery: You might have expected to find discovery in opportunity creation. I understand why you would believe it should come earlier. The truth, however, is that establishing that a client needs better results is shallow, check-the-box discovery. Capturing opportunities in B2B sales requires a deeper discovery, one that addresses both the root causes of the prospective client's difficulties, and the changes the client will need to make to improve their poor results.

Determining the Investment: If your prospective client sees the required investment for the first time when you hand over your proposal, you've made a mistake. Once you know what is necessary, you must determine the appropriate investment. It's better to have this conversation earlier than to surprise your contacts with a number beyond their willingness to pay or their budgetary constraints.

Presentations and Proposals: At some point, you will present your plan to help your prospective client improve their results. There is never a reason to provide a presentation and a proposal if you haven't already vetted it to make certain you have something your client can say *yes* to. The proposal should include the investment you have already agreed on earlier in the conversation.

Negotiation: Even though you have addressed the investment, you should always be prepared to handle a negotiation when the bean counters ask you to sharpen your pencil (even though no one uses pencils anymore). Being able to agree to, say, a larger commitment or a longer contract or something else you value more than the concession is a fundamental sales skill.

Use data and technology to its fullest potential

The biggest opportunity companies have when compared to traditional companies is the abundance of data and the ease to introduce technology to track it and keep it organized.

Here's some interesting products that can make a huge difference to your sales:

- Sales flare – of course – can help you with perfectly keeping track of your customers without inputting any data. It tracks recurring revenue like no other CRM, can send automated email sequences/flows, and has the closest possible integration with your G Suite or Office 365 inbox and calendar.
- Intercom is the best built live chat and support system around. You can also use it to send onboarding emails, show product tours, and much more.
- Segment can help you track and organize your data across apps with a minimal amount of work. Track things once, use the data everywhere.
- Acute is our tool of choice when tracking customer feedback. It links up feedback with people, essentially visualizing the connection between Intercom and Github for us.
- RingBlaze is one of the best business phone systems. It offers multiple features like call recording, group calling, auto attendant, etc. It also offers a direct call widget which you can integrate on your website. This widget can let customers connect with you directly in just a click.
- Last but not least, Zapier is what you need to integrate things across tools.

There's obviously many more products around, but those are some of the key ones we use ourselves to stay maximally organized in sales.

Things Every Manager Should Know about the Sales Process

1. Sales Mentality—Take Time to Understand the How Salespeople Think

2. Buyer's Journey—Learn Your Customers' Pain Points and How Your Solution Can Help Them

3. Sales Learning Curve—Prepare for Productivity Dips and Get Familiar with Common Mistakes

CHAPTER FOURTEEN

Social Media Marketing

Social media marketing is the use of social media platforms to connect with your audience to build your brand, increase sales, and drive website traffic. This involves publishing great content on your social media profiles, listening to and engaging your followers, analyzing your results, and running social media advertisements. The major social media platforms (at the moment) are Facebook, Instagram, Twitter, LinkedIn, Pinterest, YouTube, and Snapchat.

There are also a range of social media management tools that help businesses to get the most out of the social media platforms listed above. For example, Buffer is a platform of social media management tools, which can help you achieve success with your social media marketing. Whether you want to build a brand or grow your business, we want to help you succeed.

Social media marketing first started with publishing. Businesses were sharing their content on social media to generate traffic to their websites and, hopefully, sales. But social media has matured far beyond being just a place to broadcast content. Nowadays, businesses use social media in a myriad of different ways. For example, a business that is concerned about what people are saying about its brand would monitor social media conversations and response to relevant mentions (social media listening and engagement). A business that wants to understand how it's performing on social media would analyze its reach, engagement, and sales on social media with an analytics tool (social media analytics). A business that wants to reach a specific set of audience at scale would run highly-targeted social media ads (social media advertising).

Benefits of social media marketing: With such widespread usage and versatility, social media is one of the most effective free channels for marketing your business today. Here are some of the specific benefits of social media marketing:

Humanize your business: Social media enables you to turn your business into an active participant in your market. Your profile, posts, and interactions with users form an approachable persona that your audience can familiarize and connect with, and come to trust.

Drive traffic: Between the link in your profile, blog post links in your posts, and your ads, social media is a top channel for increasing traffic to your website where you can convert visitors into customers.

Generate leads and customers: You can also generate leads and conversions directly on these platforms, through features like Instagram/Facebook shops, direct messaging, call to action buttons on profiles, and appointment booking capabilities.

Increase brand awareness: The visual nature of social media platforms allows you to build your visual identity across vast audiences and and improve brand awareness. And better brand awareness means better results with all your other campaigns.

Build relationships: These platforms open up both direct and indirect lines of communication with your followers through which you can network, gather feedback, hold discussions, and connect directly with individuals.

Social media marketing strategy

A successful social media marketing strategy will look different for every business, but here are the things they will all have in common:

Knowledge of your audience: What platforms they use, when they go on them and why, what content they like, who else they're following, and more.

Brand identity: What is the message you want to convey to your audience? How do you want them to feel when viewing your content?

Content strategy: While there is a level of spontaneity on social, you'll need a structured content strategy to be able to have a consistent voice and produce quality content regularly.

Analytics: Quantifiable insights will inform your strategy, including who you're reaching, the right content to share, the best times to post, and more.

Regular activity: Social media is a real-time platform. If you want to use it to grow your business, you need to post regularly, stay on top of engagements with your business, engage back, keep up with trends, and maintain accurate profiles.

Inbound approach: Don't use social media to pitch your business. Focus on adding value through useful and interesting content and building up those around you. This, in turn, will organically promote your business and others will promote it for you.

Preparing your social media marketing plan

Now that you know the essentials of a social media marketing strategy, it's time to put it into action. Your social media marketing plan is the roadmap to carrying out your strategy. It puts structure around your efforts so you can measure your success and make sure you're spending your resources wisely. Here's how to create your social media marketing plan:

Choose your platforms: Choose based on your target audience, platforms popular for your industry, as well as your bandwidth. Only take on the number of platforms you can actively keep up with. You can always start with one and then add on more slowly as you get the hang of them.

Set goals and objectives: These should be simple and task-like to start, like post once a day for a month, get your profiles set up, or do a competitive analysis. Once you get into a rhythm and gather insights, you'll be able to set more specific and strategic goals like increase your following by X% or publish X [content types you've found your audience likes] per month.

Report and adjust regularly: Use each platform's analytics to identify which posts generate the most engagement, whether you're getting more followers, and to see your audience demographics. Harness and scale up what works and nix what doesn't.

Listening and Engagement

As your business and social media following grow, conversations about your brand will also increase. People will comment on your social media posts, tag you in their social media posts, or message you directly. People might even talk about your brand on social media without letting you know. So you will want to monitor social media conversations about your brand. If it's a positive comment, you get a chance to surprise and delight them. Otherwise, you can offer support and correct a situation before it gets worse. You can manually check all your notifications across all the social media platforms but this isn't efficient and you won't see posts that didn't tag your business's social media profile. You can instead use a social media listening and engagement tool that aggregates all your social media mentions and messages, including posts that didn't tag your business's social media profile. Today, it's more important than ever to meet customers where they are. We live much of our lives on social media and expect the brands we use to be there too. Our customers are as global as our far flung friends and family and the same tools that help us stay in touch with our loved ones, help 1Password stay engaged with the people who interact with us. Engagement is more than just marketing. It's lending a helping hand when things go awry, keeping the conversation going when problems are solved, and spreading the good word about what we're up to and where folks can come say hi. The conversations we have on Twitter, Facebook, Google+, Instagram, YouTube, Reddit.

Social Media Marketing Resources

Social media platforms are always evolving. When Facebook first started, people can only share text updates. Now, there are so many content formats such as images, videos, live videos, and Stories. Hence, social media marketing is always changing, too. We want to help you stay up-to-date with all the latest changes and strategies to succeed on social media. Here are a few resources to get you started:

Social Media Marketing Blog: Buffer's social media marketing blog covers the latest social media strategies and tools for Facebook, Instagram, Twitter, and more.

Social Media Marketing Guide: The complete beginner's guide to creating a social media marketing plan, for those brand new to social media and looking for a straightforward way to start.

Social Media Listening and Engagement Guide: Here's why we think social media listening and engagement is so important and how you can overcome the challenges to developing a successful strategy.

Social Media Analytics Guide: There's a wealth of information and insights in your social media data. Here are seven simple, quick, and actionable social media analytics tips.

Social Media Advertising Guide: There's so much to learn with social media advertising. It's difficult to know where or how exactly to get started. Here's everything marketers need to know about advertising on social media.

CHAPTER FIFTEEN

Top Sales Secrets

Sales is much more than providing the customer with the goods, in exchange for money. Sales involve a relationship not only between the sales representative and the customer, but the company and the customer. There are many traits that customers look for in not only products, but in sales people also. No one is born a salesperson. No one has a special gift that makes customers buy products or services. Everyone can, however, learn how to sell successfully. By learning to communicate with customers, build lead lists, and sell the company's services with authority, anyone can be a successful salesperson.

In my experience, the very best and most effective sales leaders are the ones who are always focused on what they can do to help their salespeople. They know that when all the members of the team have what they need to be successful, they themselves as the managers are also successful. They take a "you-focused approach." Such an approach helps them better understand the team as they interact with and support it. This is the single best approach to managing a sales team. Leaders need to sell their ideas, be competitive, and display the soft skills of focus and responsibility. Still, there's more to being a leader than just being a good salesperson.

Consider this example. There was a salesman who was a great problem solver and good at listening. Upon becoming a leader, he had to become a good problem solver for *others*, not only for himself. Did he have the ability and willingness to help others? In the end, he quit and found another sales position. He was not willing to invest as much in other people as he was in himself. Leaders must take on mentoring responsibilities. They need to have vision and resilience. Plus, their working environment is different. A shift from the high-pressure, ego-driven sales floor to the steady routine of management can be too jarring for some sellers. Whether this change is manageable comes down to personality, values, and what the individual finds important. Having worked in sales, top performers know what works on the sales floor. But, they might not have the broader perspective that a good leader needs.

Create a Connection: This is one strategy most leaders put on the top of their list as the most effective management strategy. Employees always work best when they can trust their leader. Get to know each of your team members – their goals, likes, dislikes, etc. Match those items with the objectives of the organization so they always know how they are affecting the overall company, and how their actions at work will help achieve their personal goals. You can create a connection by listening and sharing personal feelings and stories about their personal life, and by having a sense of humor.

Lead from the Front: Other leaders believe that success is achieved through leading from the front. Leaders need to take a proactive, rather than reactive approach to maximizing the impact of sales manager and rep performance. Leading from the front is another way of saying to lead by example. How can you encourage your employees to do something if you won't do it yourself? Thus, you should lead in the front. Embrace this role, especially during the more difficult tasks. That way, you help develop the understanding that this task isn't as insurmountable as it may seem.

Use Sales Gamification: Sales Gamification was also a top choice for sales development leaders. Friendly peer competition, badges, and leaderboards have been shown to help onboard new sales reps. A business development manager can use sales Gamification with new sales reps to engage them and boost productivity. Competition is fierce in the talent market. In an environment where workers can move fluidly from one opportunity to the next with little downtime, companies need a strong focus on engagement. Actually, the budget for prizes does not have to be substantial. Movie tickets or dinner outings for two are ideal for showing recognition because they offer experiences, rather than material goods. One more tip on Gamification is to remember that public recognition is always better and more memorable than material rewards.

Permanently Train and Review: Practice and constant training are the best way to improve results for a team. In fact, this was high on the list of tips for sales management for many of the leaders we interviewed. Practice, practice, practice. Your team needs to create their playbooks, and you must constantly review them. Once that is done, put on your "training hat and make sure your team knows the scripts/talk tracks inside and out. Listen to calls, provide feedback using the commend/recommend/commend model. When coaching, ask questions using the well, better, different model—what do you think you did well; areas you could have done better; and what do you need to do differently. Finally, managers need to create behavior plans and establish the behaviors/activities needed each hour or day to succeed. If you do the behaviors the results come.

Adopt Just-In-Time Training (JITT): Companies need to ramp up sales development reps quickly and make sure they are productive. Most of the time, they cannot afford to spend two months just for training. This is where just-in-time training comes in. Just-In-Time Training or JIIT is a type of training where information or solutions are given to trainee's right when they need them. Sometimes, this concept is also referred to as just-in-time learning. Just-in-time training helps employers and employees alike see that training is a constant thing. In today's fast-paced business environment employees want and need training that can be easily accessed and quickly consumed the moment it's needed on the job. For sales teams, this becomes a number one requirement. The ability to learn just in time, as well as to receive timely feedback, for example, on their sales pitch, are helping companies significantly increase their sales KPIs.

Opt for Live Talks vs. Digital: Technology needs to make our lives easier, not to replace our ability to be more productive. Sales coaching, or any kind of training for that matter, is best done in person. If you have a personnel issue, there is not a better way to miscommunicate and dilute your message than by sending an email, text, or instant message. In its basic form, it is cowardice to avoid a live talk for personnel matters. Don't take the easy way out and don't be lazy. Your best impact is to always talk in person or to pick up the phone. Although digital communication is definitely useful in many ways, face-to-face communication is more abundant in the information. It relies on your interpersonal skills to manage relationships.

Implement a Culture of Empowerment: Empowering people to make an impact on the business and making their own decisions is also high on the list of tips from sales development leaders. Installing a culture of empowerment leads to a positive, high-performing team. When a level of empowerment is high, your ability to retain talent and achieve quota is also high.

Know the Difference between Micromanaging and Accountability: Effective leaders know how to steer clear of micro-management, or excessive involvement while making sure there is accountability for each team member. Although the border can be vague, there is a clear difference between micromanaging and holding people accountable. The difference can be seen in the control over the overall work quality. One of the great challenges with teams today is that we have lost sight of accountability, prompting people to confuse accountability with micro-managing. I see this on a daily basis, leaders who fear holding people accountable because they don't want to be perceived as micro-managers. I also see employees who defend their lack of accountability by falsely claiming as the self-proclaimed company spokesman—'We are being micromanaged.' It's a chronic problem that needs to be corrected today. Giving feedback in a professional but unflinching manner can ensure you aren't crossing that line of being a micromanager. Being able to hold the right people accountable without being too controlling is an underrated but valuable part of having leadership skills.

Create a Clear Path to Advancement: One of the significant problems in sales development organizations in the industry is that people feel stuck in their career. Salespeople want to know that their work experience will lead up to something eventually. Thus, leaders need to make sure there is a clearly defined career path to sales or management. A best practice is to create a tiered promotion system, where people can move up in-role based on performance and skill development. The final tier should define someone as 'sales-ready. Putting people in control over their own career progression improves retention and performance as well.

Be Compassionate: Sales leaders can't be expected to keep their team motivated if they're burned out themselves. Sales development leaders to be compassionate to their team and to themselves. It's tough to stay motivated when rejection happens frequently throughout the day. My suggestion to sales leaders is to fall back on self-compassion—and hopefully compassion within your sales team/corporate culture. To draw on self-compassion, give yourself a break regularly. Being a compassionate leader isn't only a feel-good approach to business development. In fact, there are a lot of benefits to businesses that have a compassionate leader among their ranks. More compassion in the organization benefits not only the employees but also your revenue. Compassionate leaders make compassionate employees. In turn, positively influenced employees have better interactions and relationships with prospective customers. Consequently, this will attract more people to transact with your business.

Constantly Interview: Making interviews a constant is one strategy to keep your sales development reps awake during work hours. Albeit, there is a chance it will keep them awake at night as well. As the leader of a sales team, it's important to let your team know that you're always on the lookout. It's not so much that you're always hiring, but that there's an unspoken threat – if they don't keep up, they can be replaced. This sense of being at the edge of your seat makes your sales reps more vigilant. Thus, they'll be on their A-game more often than not with this strategy.

LEARN FROM YOUR TOP SELLERS AND IMPROVE YOUR BUSINESS: Perhaps more than any other profession, there is a perception of a "secret formula" in being a good seller. Sometimes it comes from natural intuition. More often, it's gained through careful observation and experience. The art of selling is a mixture of soft skills and hard results that make a recipe for success. While not all good sellers become great leaders, they offer many valuable lessons for leadership. Smart leaders will use these skills to improve themselves and the rest of their sales team.

Sell benefits, not features: The biggest mistake entrepreneurs make is in focusing on what their product or service is. Rather, it's what it does that's important, says Tracy. A health-food product contains nutrients that are good for the body. That's what it is. What the product does is make the customer thinner, more energetic, and able to accomplish more with less sleep, he explains. Always concentrate on how your product will benefit your customer.

Sell to the people most likely to buy: Your best prospects have a keen interest in your product or service and the financial resources to purchase it. They are the ones who will buy most quickly. If you're selling photo-copy machines, don't try to sell to people who have never bought one before. Sell to those who already have one, or to those you know would be interested in buying one. Show them how yours is superior.

Target your material toward a specific audience: These days, it's not possible to understand and meet the needs of every potential customer. You have a selling advantage and come across as believable when your sales materials are tightly targeted to specific audiences.

Use testimonials: People might not believe your product or service can do what you say it will. You can overcome this disbelief by having a past or present customer praise you and your company. Testimonials are usually written in the customer's own words, are surrounded by quotation marks, and are attributed to the individual. They can be used in sales letters, brochures and advertisements.

Two Big Ideas: Maybe you're wondering how to make sure that *you* are following this you-focused approach. Begin by accepting two big ideas.

- First and foremost, your relationships with team members matter a whole lot more than your job title.
- Second, those relationships always depend on them *believing* you are serving the team.

Taken together, these ideas suggest that your primary goal as a sales leader has nothing to do with whether people are positioned "above" or "below" you in the organization, whether salespeople are obliged to do what you say, or whether anyone gives you credit for anything. Instead, your primary goal must be to make sure your salespeople know and trust, deep down, that you have their interests at heart and will do whatever it takes to support them and help them succeed. Remember: you win when they win. Unfortunately, this "you-focused" approach is typically *not* the default setting for sales managers. Most traditional organizations have a hierarchal, top-down organizational chart where the person at the top says, "I am in charge—so do what I say." The most effective leaders, however, invert this chart. They say, in essence, "Hey, regardless of what the job titles says, you don't work for me. I actually work for all of you. What can I do to make your jobs easier, and what can I do to support your goals?" In other words, the cornerstone of their management style is their attitude of service to the other members of the team—and they mean it. It is absolutely essential.

If you are authentic about this, if you are comfortable in your own skin, if you are willing to do what it takes to support your team in the most effective way, then you won't be tempted to hide behind your job title or "pull rank." On the other hand, if you're not willing to support the team and you're more interested in exerting authority based on your position, the team will pick up on this—and they will lose respect for you in your role as leader. Our experience is that too many leaders, in sales and elsewhere, manage with their ego rather than taking on an attitude of service. This is a big mistake. Your management role should not be the source for fulfilling the needs of your ego.

Sales Management a Reality: Constantly remind yourself that your #1 job is to make sure that your individual team members are succeeding. You need to set up a plan to accomplish that. When creating that plan, bear in mind one of the many common reasons people leave a company is they don't respect their manager. Note: It's not disrespecting the institution of management—they don't respect a specific individual. This is not the path you want your sales team to follow!

- Think of the three people on your team you would most like to retain.
- Ask yourself: How much do those people respect you, right now?
- Ask yourself: Do they respect you enough to stick around for another year—or do you get a little closer to losing them with every passing day?
- Ask yourself: Do they each know, on a personal level, that you fully support them?
- Ask yourself: If a competitor came along tomorrow morning and tried to recruit them, what would happen?

With honest answers to those questions in mind, take a step back the next time you're inclined to give an order without any kind of consultation, issue an ultimatum, or end a sentence with. This behavior is not supporting the team it's fixating on your own ego and job title.

Notice, too, that a "you-based" management style doesn't mean you don't make decisions. It does mean, though, that you explain the reasoning behind decisions you are considering making ... and get buy-in from the team. Service-oriented leaders in the sales arena take the opportunity to know, and pay attention to, their salespeople – as individuals. Just as buyers and customers need attention and support over time, so do your salespeople. Send the message to your salespeople that says you really are there to serve them. And mean it! So make sure you're paying attention to the needs of each member of your team. Ask directly, in one-on-one conversations, what you can do to help them succeed. Really listen to their answers, and do your best to take action on what you hear. Avoid the temptation to use your position as a shield against criticism, or as justification for decisions you make without talking to those whom the decisions affect. Managers who use their position on the organizational chart to pump up their own position or to win arguments inevitably end up losing good people they could have kept. They're leading with the title, instead of leading with the relationship.

A well-defined sales process increases sales revenues: Far too often competent salespeople are counted upon to channel their own activities into the areas that will produce the biggest and quickest wins. But, left to their own devices, sales people generally don't develop and pursue a formal plan for moving a prospect interaction forward toward a sale. Instead, they end up 'dancing around' hoping they will get to their chosen point on the dance-floor (the sale). This is normally unsuccessful because, as recent research from The Results Corporation plc shows, the average prospect says "No" seven times before saying "Yes" and over 80 percent of sales people give up after the first "No." They carry on dancing. When their efforts don't pay off quickly, even capable sales people tend to get discouraged. They may spend longer hours struggling to meet their sales quotas, working less efficiently. The details of what goes wrong differ for each sales person, but the net result is always the same: wasted time, which fails to produce high quality sales, and consequently increases the cost of sales. For VP's of sales, sales directors and managers, this means that it's absolutely vital to develop a comprehensive, realistic and step-by-step sales process - a clear outline of what the sales people are expected to do. It's only when such an outline is in place that sales management is in a position to monitor the sales force's activity, its progress and results. Only then is the stage set for transformative performance improvements.

Focus sales people's priorities and time on core 'high-yield' selling activities: Focusing the efforts of a sales team towards a common goal that creates value for the customer, the organisation and the employee is the best way to optimize the activities of a sales team. Time is a huge constraint on sales people's activities. Any extra effort that can be achieved must be channeled into productive activities or it will mostly be wasted. Frequently two main pitfalls dilute the activities of even experienced sales people: Firstly, they simply aren't doing enough, and secondly, but equally important, sales people often aren't clear about how to identify the prospects most likely to have a genuine need for their product or service. Sales people who lack a disciplined, future-oriented plan for generating new contacts and sales, often find themselves spending more time attending to 'urgent' activities rather than 'important' activities that will develop their business. Having a clear focus on 'high-yield' activities will improve sales people's productively, and reduce time spent on unimportant non-productive tasks.

Use every means possible to expand and encourage self-belief among sales people: The saying is true: Whatever you believe you can do, you will; and whatever you believe you can't do you won't. Like everyone, sales people hold stubbornly to private beliefs about themselves and the people they work with; beliefs that can have an enormous impact, either positive or negative, on their sales performance. Yet, while most sales managers and team leaders grasp the concept of activity management, skills and knowledge development, etc., far too many feel powerless to help their sales people turn their negative beliefs into positive ones. Those who do tackle beliefs and are able to change their sales people's self-limiting beliefs into empowering ones make a remarkable difference to people's achievements and successes. Inspiring and encouraging people to strive and aim higher is one of the most significant and yet simple ways to help sales people towards higher levels of performance.

Select and develop sales managers and leaders who can inspire, develop and truly lead the sales people: The single-most common mistake that organisations make is promoting their number one sales person into the role of sales manager, thereby depriving themselves in a single stroke of their best producer and hamstringing their sales force with an ineffective manager. The skills required for managing, mentoring and developing a sales team are totally different to those required for selling. As a result, many newly-promoted sales managers become casualties - they struggle in the role, their people struggle too, and the manager often leaves the organisation in order to return to pure sales role.

Selecting, preparing, training, and appointing sales managers and sales leaders is a crucial and pivotal activity for executives and directors. Doing this right makes everything possible; getting it wrong produces havoc and failure. The majority of sales managers say they do not have sufficient time to train and develop their sales teams. They are so focused on sales results and so accustomed to achieving success through their personal pursuit that they overlook their greatest potential source of power: the power to increase sales performance by developing their people. Even when they do recognise the importance of developing their sales people, many sales managers find that they lack the skills and resources to do it effectively. It then becomes easier 'not to bother'. To make matters worse, most sales teams consist of a number of individuals with differing levels of experience and ability, so the whole issue of team development becomes too daunting to contemplate.

Common Sales Process Mistakes

Let's take a look at some common mistakes made when developing sales processes. Avoiding these will help you create a sales process ideal for both your team and customers.

Leaving Sales Process Steps Open to Interpretation: It's essential to define specific, concrete actions that move your business's prospects from one stage to the next. If you don't identify these triggers, your sales team might come away with a less than accurate understanding of what is and isn't working for prospects, potentially causing them to mishandle part of the process. Once you define your sales process, document, share, and practice it with your team. Role-play exercises to drive home the valuable techniques your team should take away from each step.

Expecting One Sales Methodology to Be the Silver Bullet: While some teams choose to stick with and follow one methodology closely, others prefer to study several popular sales methodologies and combine bits and pieces they find useful from each. Regardless of which approach you take, it's a good idea to stay aware of what's new and changing over time. As the needs and desires of buyers and your business change, different approaches, methodologies, and ways of managing your sales process will fall into and out of favor. On that note, it's important to remember your entire sales process is also ever-changing.

Forgetting Your Sales Process Will Always be a Work in Progress: Your sales process is never complete or perfect and should always be a work in progress. So, in addition to consistently measuring your success, you should also have check-ins with your reps. These check-ins help uncover any major issues or red flags with regards to your process. Remember, continually developing and improving your sales process will make your work more straightforward and improve your customers' interactions and experiences with your salespeople and business as a whole.

Not Aligning Your Sales Plays with Your Sales Process: Creating a sales process is futile if you don't align your sales plays with the process. The plays each rep must take at every step should be written down for future use. This is where a sales playbook comes in. For example, in the prospecting stage, you might typically send up to three emails to each prospect before qualifying them. Write down those emails and keep them in a shared location where everyone in your team can access them. Your sales playbook can be a formal PDF document or you can create one in a tool such as Sales Hub. By marrying your sales plays with your sales process, you can ensure that your sales organization is as efficient and effective as possible.

Leaving Marketing Out of the Loop: Marketing needs to know what's happening in your sales organization — which prospects have been proven to close, which industries are less profitable, and which market segments have potential. You want your marketing team to have all of this information so that they can better supplement each part of the process. For instance, they can provide better prospects and better lead nurturing materials — and when it's time to continue nurturing the customer, they can even take that off your hands by creating drip campaigns on your behalf. Marketing and sales alignment is critical to any organization, and that's no different when creating a profitable sales process. You can schedule monthly meetings with your marketing organization, or you can asynchronously stay aligned using an all-in-one solution such as HubSpot, where both marketing and sales tools live in one platform.

Centering the Process on Closing Deals: While sales is about closing deals, it's always about providing value first and foremost — which will hopefully end in a closed deal down the line. Even if a prospect doesn't seem like they want to purchase, you must keep providing value at every step of the process if their business needs can be solved by your product. When your sales reps research the prospect's business, they're not just looking at company size and leadership boards. They're looking for the problem that prospect is experiencing so that they can deliver a pitch that makes it hard to pass on the solution. Center your process on providing value every step on the way and not just on meeting quota and closing deals.

Forgetting to Measure KPIs: Not tracking key sales metrics or not measuring KPIs is an easy way for your sales process to become ineffective. Don't forget to measure KPIs after creating or adjusting your sales process to understand what's going well and what's not. While the focus shouldn't be on numbers only, this will help you understand your success. You can then dig deeper into the data. You can keep track of these KPIs automatically using a sales dashboard like the one included in Sales Hub. Your CRM might also provide basic performance metrics, which you can then use to adjust your existing sales process.

Creating and mapping a sales process will help your sales team close more deals and convert more leads. This will also ensure your team provides every prospect with a consistent experience that's representative of your brand. Follow these steps to create and map a sales process tailored to your business, sales team, and customers to boost conversions and build lasting relationships today.